Navigating the maze of managing people.

If You Have Employees,
Really
You Need This Book

Jerry Osteryoung, Ph.D. & Timothy J. O'Brien, M.S.

If You Have Employees, You Really Need This Book!

Cover Photograph:
Taken at P.A.T. Live,
Professionally Answered Telephones
Tallahassee, FL www.patlive.com

Photograph by: Larry Coltharp

Book Layout & Design by: Stacy L. Bagley
"Because of Stacy we have a book. No Stacy, no book.....thank you."
-Jerry & Tim

If You Have Employees, You Really Need This Book!
Library of Congress Control Number: 2010922928
Osteryoung, Jerry
O'Brien, Timothy J.
If You Have Employees, You Really Need This Book!/Jerry Osteryoung
and Timothy J.O'Brien;
ISBN 978-1-4507-0574-5
BUSINESS & ECONOMICS / Human Resources & Personnel
Management BUS030000
First Printing: March 2010
10 9 8 7 6 5 4 3 2 1
Published by ISMPI, Inc.
3023 Shannon Lakes N. Suite #102, Tallahassee, FL 32309
© 2010 by Jerry Osteryoung and Timothy J. O'Brien
Manufactured in the United States of America.
All rights reserved.
For information about, "If You Have Employees, You Really Need This
Book!" please contact Jerry Osteryoung and/or Timothy J. O'Brien
jerry@osteryoungobrien.com
tim@osteryoungobrien.com
http://www.osteryoungobrien.com

Dedication

We dedicate this book to the more than 3,000 entrepreneurs, business owners, associations, and managers who have opened their businesses to us, so that others can learn from their experiences.

– Jerry & Tim

About the Authors

"The Professor"

Jerome ("Jerry") S. Osteryoung, Ph.D. is the Director of Outreach Services of the Jim Moran Institute for Global Entrepreneurship in the College of Business at Florida State University. He is the Jim Moran Professor of Entrepreneurship (Emeritus); and a Professor of Finance (Emeritus). Dr. Osteryoung is an internationally known speaker and a highly in demand, business coach.

"The Practitioner"

Tim O'Brien, M.S., is a successful entrepreneur from Tallahassee, Florida, the Director of The Institute for Stress Management & Performance Improvement, and a Life Member of The International Society for Performance Improvement. For 14 years, Tim wrote a column for Knight Rider News Service and has published more than 400 articles.

Table of Contents

Table of Contents

Agreement of Use

Introduction

Whether you own a business or manage a profit or non-profit corporation, your number one concern must be your staff. There is no higher calling than being a manager. Your staff spends more time with you than they do with their families. They also rely on you for motivational support and guidance in many ways.

Learning how to be a great manager comes from continuing to learn new skills and polishing your existing ones. We have structured this book to help you become the best manager possible and to help you avoid costly management mistakes.

If You Have Employees, You (Really) Need This Book is an action-oriented guide that helps you select, motivate, coach, train and retain a high energy and effective staff.

The book's 13 chapters navigate you through the maze of dealing with employees through its precise and direct format, which includes easy to follow models, practices, and forms.

You also have access to a content rich companion website *(www.osteryoungobrien.com)* that expands on many of the topics in the book. The website has PDF forms and resource links that allow you to get the maximum benefit from the book.

Use this book for selecting key employees to insure that an applicant is your type of employee. Use it to motivate teams, handle problem employees, and get critical buy-in for your projects.

Whether you are a business owner, manager, or CEO, you can use it as a quick reference guide for ideas, methods, and resources. You and your managers can benefit from the key points given for motivating individual employees and teams. Your teams can use it as a guide for planning their work, as well as using the suggestions provided, on how to avoid conflict and resolve disputes.

All of your departments will find this book an invaluable

guide to improving the productivity of the people they work with and manage.

You will find that this book pays for itself a thousand times over with just one bad hire avoided, one great employee retained, or one major benchmark reached by a team.

How To Use This Book

You will find this book most valuable if you read the chapters in the order they are written and complete all the exercises. After you have read each chapter, develop a plan implementing that material. Of course, if you have a specific problem or question you can refer to the table of contents or the index to address your concern immediately.

Progressing through the book sequentially, however, will improve your team, your company, and your managerial skills.

Let's get started!

"Find associates with impeccable character
and motivation, and pay them very well."
— Jim Moran on the secret to his success.

Chapter 1

Selecting Employees

● ●

Chapter At-A-Glance

By the end of this chapter you will know:

- How to identify the qualities and characteristics of a great employee.
- How to start your search for the right people to join your workforce.
- How to administer the proper procedure for interviewing and assessing a potential employee
- What to avoid saying /asking during an interview.
- How to check out references with a two-level process.
- What a 90-day probation is and why it is important.

Business owners and managers exist and thrive because of their employees. They function as the interface between each customer and the business. In order to grow, or even just exist, you must have your business adequately staffed. Trying to grow your business without sufficient resources, including people, is a recipe for disaster as customer service will be destroyed. While it is very easy to say businesses need great employees, finding them can prove difficult. Because of this, some business owners keep the same people and processes they've employed since they started their business, somehow expecting the business to magically grow. They repeat the same strategies expecting different results. Growing a business is a challenge, but not

1

taking the steps to meet that challenge doesn't make it easier. In order to grow your business you need dedicated employees who are also willing to grow.

Before you worry about finding new employees, look at how you are treating your existing employees. It is estimated that it costs about 1.5 times the salary of the old employee to replace them with a new employee. Much of this cost is related to training a new employee and getting him or her up to speed. Consider home-growing the qualified staff that you need. For example, if you are looking for a salesman, you may want to set up a training program that will teach the requisite skills to existing employees.

Retraining is not always practical, however. If you are considering enlarging an employee's responsibility, think not so much as to what is in the best interest of the firm, but rather whether or not the job responsibility will fit within the comfort zone and skill set of the employee. Frequently, it may be beneficial to bring some new help in to do the job rather than trying to force a new role onto an already overworked and non-skilled employee.

■ Qualities of a Great Employee ■

You should not search for good employees - you must locate great people to work with you. Experience is not the most important factor. The critical attributes to look for when hiring new associates are character, motivation, people skills, and intelligence.

Character includes attributes like punctuality, honesty, diligence, and perseverance. It is impossible to train someone who has bad character qualities to perform with good character. You cannot change the character of an individual in the workplace. Therefore, you need to hire people of great character.

Motivation is also important in hiring workers.

Chapter 1 – Critical Attributes

People are either motivated or they are not. We just cannot take lazy individuals and inspire them to be motivated to do a great job for us. Rather, we need to hire motivated people.

Finally, you need to make sure you find employees who really enjoy dealing with people. It is very difficult to take an introverted employee and turn him or her into a people-person. Especially in retailing or other businesses that deal with the public, your entire staff must really enjoy serving and helping customers. Even positions which do not require interfacing with customers need to be filled by those who can work well with others.

Experience is not critical because experience is one thing you can give your staff over time. We can normally teach job skills, but it is almost impossible to instill passion and motivation. While it may take longer to train motivated, but inexperienced, employees, they will be much more effective in the long run than potential associates who

Critical Attributes

- Character
- Motivation
- People Skills
- Intelligence

have job knowledge but no motivation.

Another core attribute to be considered when looking for new employees is intelligence. Smart associates will stimulate your organizations growth. If you limit your employees to those who are not as intelligent as you, then you will significantly inhibit the growth and excitement of your business.

Hire bright people, even if they are brighter than you. You must select intelligent people that will add value to your organization. Without exception, those firms that are growing rapidly in terms of sales and profits seem also to be the ones that have incredibly bright people in their organizations.

Chapter 1 – Finding the Right People

━ Finding the Right People ━

One idea you might consider is to have a referral program for existing employees to recommend a new employee. Firms frequently pay between $200 and $500 for each employee hired. It is worth while to pay a small amount (between $25 to $50) to employees just for turning in the name of a qualified candidate. This encourages your staff to be always on the lookout for new employees.

Another method of finding viable potential associates is letting your network of acquaintances and friends know of your need. Explicitly tell them what qualities you are looking for in your staff. This is one of the most effective means of finding new employees.

If you are looking for part-time workers, consider placing flyers on college campuses and other well-frequented places. Many college students want to work, but just do not know where to go for a job.

Ways To Locate Good People

- Referral Programs
- Tell Friends, Acquaintances, and Customers
- Post Flyers in "Hot Spots"
- Employment Services
- Classified Ads

Using an employment service is another way to find great employees. While this may cost 20 or 30% of the employee's first year's salary, these services can be very good at finding employed individuals who are looking for a new job. Also, they do the preliminary interviewing so you do not have to go through this tedious process. If you choose to use an employment firm make sure they offer reduced fees in the event the employee stays for a limited amount of time.

Chapter 1 – Recruiting

Recruiting From Other Companies

Ask Yourself. . .

Suppose you see a very capable, top-notch employee working for your competitor. You feel this person would make a great employee in your business. Should you consider asking the employee if he (or she) would like to come work for you?

Think It Through. . .

In order to see this issue correctly, you must have the correct perspective. If I am competing with another entrepreneur for some new business, am I concerned about hurting the competition in making the bid or do I do the best I can to get the work? Of course, I am going to try to get the job by pricing it favorably and by providing additional services to make my bid the most attractive.

Act On It. . .

Competition is competition. Part of competition is to get the best resources you can in order to deliver great customer service. This might mean that if you get a chance to hire a great employee away from a competitor, you act on it.

Overview. . .

The question really comes down to this: does the ill-will you produce by trying to hire your competitors' key employees outweigh the opportunity to pursue and hire some great employees? The decision to hire a competitor's employee is not one of ethics, but one of finding and hiring the best talent.

Chapter 1 – What You Need

Consider using the classified section in the local newspaper, both in print and online editions. Additionally, Monster.com, CareerBuilders.com, and Craigslist.com are excellent places to look for employees outside of the local area. Make sure your ad stands out so that it will attract the attention of job seekers. Examine other ads in the section in which you wish to advertise. Would a bold headline help? Would a decorative box around the ad be an attention grabber? Do something to catch your potential prospect's eye.

Also, having respondents submit a resume rather than call will cut down on the time your staff spends in answering questions about the job.

What Do You Need?

Before looking to fill a position, clearly define what you are looking for. Take the time to write out a description of the position a new employee will fill.

- What skills must the employee have?
- What tasks will he or she have to perform?
- What do you expect from him or her? Why?

Some expectations are unrealistic or unattainable. When we have expectations like this, we set others and ourselves up for failure. Unrealistic and unattainable expectations fall into the category "non-functional" and waste time, energy, effort, resources, and emotions.

Legal Issues

It's a good idea to select basic interview questions in advance. A great rule of thumb to remember when preparing interview questions is that questions must be the same for both genders and for all races. Avoid questions about age, religion, sexual orientation and disabilities. Care should be taken as even subtle questions can be problematic. For instance, age discrimination can involve more than just a straightforward inquiry about age or date of birth. Questions about dates of education may also indicate age. Similarly, you may not ask about a candidate's willingness to work on religious holidays.

Unless it relates to ability to perform the job, questions about current health status or disabilities are also off limits. Questions about a candidate's plan for a family should also be avoided. Whether a potential employee desires to get pregnant is not a question you can ask. Additionally, you cannot ask

Avoid Like the PLAGUE!!

- Age
- Religion
- Sexual Orientation
- Disabilities
- Health Status
- Pregnancies
- Arrests or Convictions
- Financial Obligations
- Bankruptcies

about the number of children they have or who will care for them. However, it's perfectly legal to ask the candidate if he or she has any commitments that would preclude them from meeting the requirements of their job or keep them from engaging in necessary job-related travel. Design your questions to determine whether an individual is capable of performing the essential functions you have defined for the position. Phrase these questions in job-related language, and

Chapter 1 – Interviews & Assessments

Online Resources

- Because of the dynamic nature of the web, we have chosen to list web-based links and resources on our website:
  www.osteryoungobrien.com
  instead of including them in this book. This way you have access to the most up-to-date information.
- In general, whenever you have a question on any topic, do what you are probably already doing. Search at Google, Yahoo!, and Bing.

avoid making assumptions about a candidate's abilities or disabilities.

Avoid any questions about past arrests or convictions unless they are relevant to the candidate's ability to perform the job. If you have any doubts, consider conducting a background check. There are agencies that do this for a fee. Personal matters like financial obligations, bankruptcies, how long the individual has lived at their current address or whether he or she rents or owns should also be avoided.

■ Interviews & Assessments ■

Don't do all the talking. Try to spend about 80% of the interview listening to the candidate's answers. Take notes. Hiring is one of business' most critical functions. It is through hiring decisions that workers are brought in to join the team, and wrong decisions can be costly and devastating to the company's morale. Listen

Power Tip

- Listen carefully to the candidate's answers.
- Understand the answers - it's ok to ask for clarification.
- Strive for consistency with questions to each candidate.

Chapter 1 – Certainty & Meaning

carefully before you form an opinion or decide to respond. When listening and uncertain, ask questions for clarification.

Create an interview process that is the same for all candidates. Consider creating an objective assessment to determine the candidate's ability to perform necessary tasks or to test his or her knowledge. Our natural biases and filters often prohibit us from making good employment decisions. *Statistically, face-to-face interviews are only right about 14% of the time. With assessments the success rate rises to around 75%.* The cost of a bad hire is very high, but the failure rate can be significantly reduced with good pre-

Four Degrees of Certainty

1. I think I can.
2. I believe I can.
3. I know I can.
4. I do.

When asking a candidate about his or her ability to perform tasks or discussing other issues, listen to the words they use in answering. There are layers and degrees of language and meaning. Applied knowledge, confidence, and ability allow us to test and to evolve through these stages.

Three Layers of Meaning

1. I don't mind.
2. It's fine or okay.
3. I enjoy or appreciate it.

Look at these statements closely. "I don't mind," implies toleration from a self-centered position. "It's fine or okay," (with the proper tone) connotes acceptance. "I enjoy it or appreciate it, " and similar statements convey a deeper comfort level with the subject under discussion.

employment assessments.

These assessments are generally conducted on the web and the cost is between $50 and $150 per employee - a cost that will be offset many times over by hiring the right person the first time. Industry studies and turnover formulas show that each employee making minimum wage who is turned over after three months of employment will cost a company approximately $4,265.00 above any wages and benefits already paid to the employee.

If you decide to try employment assessments, the testing company will ask some of your great employees to take the assessment first and then use the results as a benchmark for any prospective employees. Smaller business owners who have a limited number of employees, making it difficult to establish benchmarks, now have no excuse. There are industry benchmarks for just about every known position and assessment-testing companies have statistically established the data for use by smaller companies.

Checking References

Do not hire a prospective associate based solely on the interview. A job interview is a controlled and artificial situation in which both sides are putting on their best face. Nor should you put much faith in exams or tests that purport to measure character. Instead, find reliable information by talking to fellow associates and prior bosses that are not used for references. References supplied by job applicants are going to be biased and should be used only as a way to find other people who know the job applicant.

Ask for three or four references, call them (discount much of what they say), and ask them each for three names of people who worked with or knew the prospective associate.

Call these references of references for a better indicator of the character and motivation of the potential associate. This technique appears to work much better in sorting out ill-motivated associates. If you have any doubts after talking to these second-level references, it is probably best to pass on the person. Those early doubts or "uh-oh" feelings are warning signals that something is not right.

Power Tip!

Some questions you may want to ask the references are:

- *Would you rehire this associate? Why or why not?*
- *How do they work with other associates?*
- *If you were going to describe this person, what are three words you would use?*
- *What are three of this person's worst attributes?*
- *What are this person's important values in life?*
- *Is there anyone else you recommend I speak with?*

These questions will help you gain an insight into the character and motivation of a prospective associate.

Bracket Your Hiring Risk

Hiring, in so many ways, is an art form, and there are no guarantees. Frequently, a new associate looks good in an interview, but just does not work out on the job. It is almost impossible to discover this until you see the person in action. We like the saying, "Hire slowly but terminate rapidly." Every employer should put new hires through a probation period during the early days of their employment.

The probation period usually lasts 90 days and should be used to gain a window into the behavior of every new employee. Do new hires get along with the team?

Chapter 1 – Bracket Your Hiring Risk

Are they self-starters or do they always need someone else to motivate them? How is their character manifested in various situations? How are their people skills?

If you observe any lapse in these qualities or if you have any doubts, you need to let the employee go. Problem employees or potential problem employees do not get better with time.

During the probationary period, you can let the employee go for any reason. If you wait until after the 90-day period, terminating an employee is much more complicated – and potentially costly. Up until the 89th day, your reason for firing can be "just cuz". On the 91st day, you need just cause.

Hiring employees involves risk, as does any situation which requires us to make decisions that have ramifications into the unknown future. Taking risks is part and parcel of business.

You should, however, limit the amount of risk that you are willing to take. For

Power Tip!

Put new employees through a 90-day probation period. During this period, you might want to look for answers to the following questions.

- Do new hires get along with the team?
- Are they self-starters or do they constantly need someone else to motivate them?
- How is their character manifested in various situations?
- How are their people skills good enough for the job?

example, if you are hiring a new sales person, you need to tell them that you will only keep them employed for three months unless they cover their salary with commissions. Bracketing risk allows you to reduce the exposure that you might incur with a new concept by setting a finite limit to the amount you wish to invest in it. With a new office manager, you might make the employment conditional on the improvement in your business' net profit by a certain date. If the employee doesn't perform, they are automatically released from employment and your risk has stopped at your chosen level. Bracketing is a very simple way to contain risky decisions.

Some entrepreneurs keep ineffective employees on past the probation period because they do not want to admit that they made a mistake in hiring. Not wanting to admit a wrong decision, however, costs them dearly over time in low morale and difficult situations. Obviously, before you let any employee go, you need to make sure that the employee understands your expectations, and you should provide some sort of counseling to address any problem areas. If employees, especially new hires, are not

---

"Are you ever wrong?"

"Are you ever wrong?" That question took Tim by surprise. He quickly recovered and answered, "Yes. I'm wrong quite often actually."

"Do you admit it to others as regularly as you should?" Tim didn't answer that one quite as fast. There were times when admitting a mistake hurt.

Consider to yourself, "Am I ever wrong?" And, "How often do I admit it?"

Accept that no one is right all the time, not even you. Tom Watson, the founder of IBM said, "to increase the success rate, double the failure rate." We all must take risks to succeed. Admit the failures, learn from them, and build on what you've learned.

given enough guidance, they are probably going to disappoint you because they are just going to be lost when it comes to performing their duties. However, if it becomes clear that the employee just will not work out, he or she should be let go.

Power Tip!

- Make sure employees get proper training.
- Address problem areas immediately.
- Make sure employees know and understand your expectations.

Chapter Wrap-Up

Chapter Wrap-Up

In this chapter you have learned:
- Employees are the key elements to growing a successful business.
- While locating great employees, make sure they have the following critical attributes:
  - Good Character
  - Motivation
  - People Skills
  - Intelligence
- To locate employees you can:
  - Use a referral program with current employees.
  - Scout from competitors employee line-up.
  - Use flyers around college campuses or other hot spots in town.
  - Use an employment service.
  - Advertise in the classifieds of newspapers, magazines, or online (ex. Craig's List).
  - Host a "Career Night" if you need a variety of types of employees.
- When interviewing avoid questions about the following topics:
  - Age
  - Race
  - Religion
  - Sexual Orientation
  - Health Status, Disabilities, and Pregnancies
  - Arrests or Convictions
  - Financial Obligations and Bankruptcies
- Only do 20% of the talking during an interview, and use the 80% left to listen.
- Create a standard interview to conduct with all potential employees. You may want to get help from an Employee Assessment Company.
- Check references from references.
- Use a 90-Day Probation Period for all new employees. If they aren't working out let them go.

Chapter 1 – Preparing for Expansion

 PDF's of these forms are available online at:
www.osteryoungobrien.com
enter code: **OST+OBR=2010**

Preparing for Expansion

Here are some questions to ask yourself before expanding your staff.

1. *What size business do I have?* _____
   _____

2. *How many employees do I need to run my business functionally
   and successfully?* _____
   _____

3. *How many employees do I already have? What job responsibilities
   do they currently have?* _____
   _____
   _____
   _____

4. *Do my current employees do their job effectively and efficiently?*
   _____

5. *How can I reorganize the company for growth?* _____
   _____

6. *Can current employees handle more responsibility or do I need to
   add a new member to the staff?* _____
   _____

Chapter 1 – Preparing for Expansion

7. What responsibilities will be expected of the new employees?___
_____
_____

8. Have I tried/Do I want to try locating potential employees through classifieds (newspapers, websites such as Monster.com, Careerbuilder.com, Craigslist.com)?_____
_____

9. Have I tried/Do I want to try locating potential employees through local colleges? _____
_____

10. Would cross training, job sharing, or job rotation fill the gaps we've identified and reduce our need for new employees?_____
_____
_____
_____

11. Are there any productivity enhancements (technology, workspace layout, adjunctive aid) that would allow our current staff to handle the perceived shortages effectively? Are those enhancements practical/effective? Would they help us fast enough? _____
_____
_____

Power Quote!

"Executives owe it to the organization and to their fellow workers not to tolerate non-performing individuals in important jobs."

-Peter Drucker

Chapter 1 – Sample Interview Questions

 PDF's of these forms are available online at:
www.osteryoungobrien.com
enter code: OST+OBR=2010

Sample Interview Questions

What are some of your long-range and short-range goals? Where do you see yourself in two to five years? _____

_____

What are some specific ways that you can make a contribution to our company? _____

What interests you about our product or service? _____

_____

How would you deal with a very difficult and controlling boss(not that we have any of these here)? _____

_____

Assume that you did not get along with a co-worker. What would you do to patch things up? _____

How will you know, or define, if you are a success at our company? _____

_____

Are you willing to travel and how much? _____

Are you willing to relocate? _____

If you could look back at your career after spending five to ten years here, what would you envision? _____

_____

What three things are most important for you in the job you are applying for? _____

_____

_____

Chapter 1 – Sample Interview Questions

What are two accomplishments you have found gratifying and why? ___
_____

*In your periodic evaluation, what factors would you like us to consider?*__
_____

How would you describe your ideal job? _____
_____

What types of job responsibilities do you find to be most frustrating? Why?
_____

Describe a project when you had to sacrifice quality for a deadline, or visa versa. How did you react to this and how did this feel to you? _____
_____

*What is your view as to your role and our role in the community?*_____
_____

Give me two improvements or suggestions you offered in your last job within the last six months? _____
_____
_____
_____

*If you disagreed with your supervisor on a specific issue, how would you handle this?*_____
_____

Describe how you would deal with an irate customer? _____
_____

*How would you handle getting different assignments from two or more bosses?*_____
_____

Chapter 1 – Take-Aways & Action Steps

Take-Aways and Action Steps

1. _____

_____

Completion Date: _____

Results: _____

_____

2. _____

_____

Completion Date: _____

Results: _____

_____

3. _____

_____

Completion Date: _____

Results: _____

_____

4. _____

_____

Completion Date: _____

Results: _____

_____

5. _____

_____

Completion Date: _____

Results: _____

_____

Chapter 2

Employee Motivation

• •

Chapter At-A-Glance

By the end of this chapter you will know:

- What your corporate culture is vs. what it needs to be.
- Why it is important to make work more enjoyable for you and your employees.
- The importance of an incentive system and why to get employee feedback.
- When it is appropriate to use monetary incentives.
- It's better to be an optimist than a pessimist in business.

If there is one common problem nearly all business owners and managers face, it is motivating employees and getting them to work together as a team. Clearly, you want to employ people who are already motivated and team players, however, frequently that just does not happen. Lack of motivation in an organization causes internal conflict. This conflict is an emotional friction; it wears on the nerves and attitudes of those affected. It can drain away excitement, enthusiasm and determination, impacting productivity negatively. To prevent this, you must find an effective way to motivate your employees.

While the concept that people need to enjoy themselves at work seems rather obvious, numerous studies have shown that workers who enjoy their jobs are more productive and have greater longevity. Too often staff members are working only for a paycheck and not because they really enjoy their job. There are a number of ways to make the workplace more enjoyable which in turn will motivate your employees.

Corporate Culture

The first step in making your workplace enjoyable is evaluating your corporate culture. In order to understand your corporate culture, you need to survey your existing employees. You can use written surveys, focus groups, or interviews. Some key questions to seek answers for are:

FYI

Corporate culture (sometimes referred to as shared values) is generally defined as the principles and practices of a business' employees.

"Is it difficult to raise a concern?"

"Is bad behavior tolerated?"

"Are the goals of the employees the same as the owner's?"

"Are ethical values supported and maintained?"

"Do you have the tools and resources you need to be successful at your job?"

"How would you describe this culture?"

After you have a handle on the existing corporate culture, assess it to see if these values serve the mission of your organization. Frequently, you will find that some of the corporate values (i.e., tolerating bad behavior) do not serve the organization. Turmoil is created in the workplace when an organization's mission and its culture are not aligned.

Once you understand your corporate culture, determine what type of culture you need to develop so that the culture is congruent and aligned with the goals of your firm. This requires the organization to change and that is tough as ingrained values are hard to alter. However, aligning corporate culture with company goals is a crucial aspect of every business. Once you understand what your corporate culture needs to be, work with your staff to change the current culture so that it is in synch with your company's goals. Work to make the changes in small steps if possible. If that doesn't work, sometimes immediate and drastic change that you commit to stick with, is the only way. Try the carrot but don't be afraid of the big stick if that is what the situation requires.

Involving Staff

One of the most effective ways to ensure your workplace is pleasant, is to simply ask your staff for suggestions. Go directly to the source and ask your employees what would make their jobs more enjoyable. We have seen requests for everything from company-wide, after-hour activities to expanded assignments. Recommendations like these are often very helpful.

By far, the most effective way to create an enjoyable workplace is to get your employees to "buy in" to your business. Create a sense of ownership among your employees. When employees

Tell them they are important, early & often!

Remember to acknowledge how important your associates are to your business. Your employee may be thinking, "I'm only a secretary."

Telling her of the difficulties you faced when she took a vacation and thanking her for the job she does around the office is a simple way of making work more enjoyable.

A single flower and a simple note saying, "We missed you," on her desk as she returns from vacation or sick leave makes a strong statement.

Chapter 2 – Employees Enjoyment

feel as though your business is also their business, the change in the way they work is significant.

At the heart of this "buy in" is communication. It is critical that you let each worker know what plans and dreams you hold for the company. By sharing information, you are really telling each worker that he or she is an integral part of the team. Use discretion in how much sensitive information you divulge. However, what and how much you share will likely depend on an individual's position in the company. If you tell someone something in confidence be sure they know it is not for sharing.

In cases where employees repeatedly perform routine tasks, minimizing monotony can make the job more enjoyable. Many offices overcome this "routine boringness" by periodically having their managers and employees alternate jobs. Financial institutions often use this method with their tellers. For employees like bank tellers, working in the same position day after day is a sure recipe for boredom. Little things like occasionally moving a teller from a desk to the drive-through help immensely. Also, suggest that workers attend to tasks in time blocks of at least 30 focused minutes; hour-long blocks are even better. This allows them to concentrate on one task at a time, maximizing productivity. If you arrange or

Do your employees enjoy their job?

With the prospect of significant worker shortages on the horizon, keeping your existing workforce satisfied and fulfilled is paramount. The key is to insure your employees truly enjoy their jobs and know that you appreciate their efforts. Tell them early in their employment and often!

- To what extent do your employees enjoy their job?

- Do they understand the importance of the role they play?

alternate the time blocks to allow the use of different skills or muscles, this will further alleviate boredom.

Do not forget to have some fun. Firms that have the highest morale and the lowest employee turnover also have the most fun. Don't take fun to mean practical jokes and horseplay; rather, think of it as meaning, "really enjoying the moment." Humorous posters that convey a lesson or goal can help.

Also important is celebrating both the successes of the business or a team and the accomplishments of each individual. In addition, birthday and anniversary celebrations are important to every one of your employees. Celebrating an achieved milestone or

Calendar

Make an "Office Celebrations Calendar."

- Set it up in a central location.
- Ask employees to add their special dates. (Don't be surprised or shocked at what they list!)
- Add your own special dates.
- This will make your employees feel important.
- It will also serve as a helpful reminder for you.

completion of a project does not need to be expensive. A smile, handshake and a thank you note for a job well done, are powerful, inexpensive, and effective when done sincerely.

Incentive Systems

The basics of incentives are to structure them based on areas that the employee can control. If the employee can only control certain costs, for instance, then the incentive should be set up around their efforts to reduce those costs without affecting quality or customer service and satisfaction.

Try to start with one

area for incentives making sure it works before you add more. A good rule of thumb when planning incentives is to address the easiest area to incentivize first. This helps build up confidence for both the business owner and the employees.

It is very useful when setting up incentives to ask employees what an appropriate incentive would be and how it could be structured. In just about every case, the employees will develop a much tougher incentive than the business owner would. Also, bringing the employees into the process increases the acceptance of the concept. It is much harder for employees to criticize what they have had a hand in developing.

After incentives are set in place, you need to watch them carefully. Sometimes incentives do not work out the way you think they will. This is normal, but you need to make changes quickly if it happens. For example, if you see employees working 110%

Setting Up An Incentive System

There are many ways to set up an incentive system including:

1. Labor Savings
2. Higher Productivity
3. Cost Savings
4. Increase in Revenues
5. Team or Group Performance
6. Overall Performance of the Business
7. Subjective
8. Combination of Above

and still not achieving the incentive, you need to adjust the incentive down. Having the bar set too high will destroy morale. Remember that incentives do not always have to be dollars. They can come in the form of recognition, an afternoon off, a better office, longer breaks, extra donuts and any other item or act your employees would consider valuable.

Chapter 2 – Put Time on Your Side

> **Put time on your side.**

Let's debunk a few myths about monetary incentives.

In our society, **money is convenience**.
Few of us still raise our own food. Few of us barter for our needs. We don't pay our utility bill with a hog. Money plays many roles depending on its use.

- Money can have power. It is energy.
- It can help heal through paying for top medical attention.
- It can help make us safe by allowing us to live in a secure neighborhood.
- It can increase health through paying for a gym membership.

One commodity that money can't buy is time.
We all have the same 24 hours each day, no more, no less. However, those with adequate income can have more free time. In our society, there is no rarer or more prized commodity than time.

- People want (but may no longer be able)to retire early.
- Employees want to work fewer hours and have weekends off.
- Time is at a premium.

Because of this, incentives which take the value of employee's discretionary time into consideration will be more effective than incentives which ignore time's value and focus only on rewarding associates monetarily.

Monetary Incentives

When dealing with monetary incentives, keep in mind that the reward needs to be given out as soon as practical. Giving out incentives once a year is too infrequent. Awarding incentives the month following of an evaluation, for example, is often best. Schedule incentive payouts close enough for employees to see the connection between extra effort and extra pay, but far enough apart to prevent adding unnecessary administrative costs.

So many entrepreneurs are plagued by confusion and guilt over holiday bonuses. It's important to keep in mind that a monetary gift should not be related to the occurrence of a holiday, but rather to the productivity of employees and the business. There is a large difference between rewarding

> **Power Quote!**
>
> *"Reward employees for work that also maximizes the business' returns."*
> **- Jerry Osteryoung**

employees because of a holiday and rewarding employees because of productivity. Having a holiday party is great and giving your staff a nice food basket is super and communicates that you care; but monetary rewards based on the company's productivity should not be connected to any holiday.

The more you can establish congruence between your workers' goals and your business' goals, the better your company will be. This congruency includes linking goals and incentive plan payouts.

Positive Leadership

Fun is something to encourage and foster. With appropriate fun and humor, the workplace becomes an enjoyable place, where people come to work, not only willingly, but also eagerly and with a sense of excitement about the day ahead. In the really fun work places, without exception, the tone is set by the leader or the business owner. Fun business owners are ones that have a sense of balance in their lives and who do not take their work too seriously. This type of attitude is contagious from the top down.

So, how can you foster a positive attitude in your workplace and yourself?

Dr. Martin Seligman of the University of Pennsylvania has spent more than 35 years studying optimists. Originally, he wanted to know why some people quit and become helpless while others, no matter what the odds, refuse to give up.

Seligman's research first led to the development of the "Learned Helplessness" model. He proved that certain behavior patterns, when habitually repeated, led to helplessness.

He then wondered, if we can learn helplessness, can we learn optimism? He discovered, yes, we can! Dr. Seligman found that how we speak to ourselves, our internal dialogue or "self talk," determines whether we are optimists or pessimists. He calls this our "explanatory style." He isolated 3 important pairs of words that make the difference. These pairs are:

1. *personal or non-personal*
2. *permanent or temporary*
3. *pervasive or specific*

Optimists describe good/positive events using personal, permanent, pervasive terms.

"Good luck always happens to me."

29

Chapter 2 – Tree Bucks

"Who'll give me tree bucks?"

Fred Beshears, owner of Simpson Nurseries in Monticello Florida, and his management staff had devised a great idea. His company supplies trees and plants to Home Depot and Lowe's, plus many other retailers throughout the country. Fred has about 150 employees who work outside, doing jobs like loading trucks or repotting plants. Not many of his employees wake up in the morning and say, "I really, really want to go work outside today in temperatures of 110 degrees." So, Fred and his two sons, Halsey and Thad, had to invent an original way to motivate their workers.

They came up with the concept of "Tree Bucks." Because attendance and punctuality are important to the business, every employee gets $10 worth of Tree Bucks each day they show up for work on time. Additionally, if employees do outstanding work, supervisors can give out additional Tree Bucks as rewards.

Twice a year, the Beshears host a cookout for all their employees. After lunch, employees sit back in their chairs and participate in an auction. The currency they use at this auction is "Tree Bucks." Fred purchases TVs, barbecue grills, bicycles, goats, video games, and a great deal more. He even auctions items such as two days off with pay or a three-day vacation trip with pay.

If the employees do not use all their Tree Bucks, they can save them and bring them back to the next auction six months later. While Tree Buck auctions may not work for every business, coming up with creative ways to motivate your staff can be incredibly effective, not to mention fun!

How will you use this concept in your business?

They describe negative/adverse events in non-personal, temporary, and specific terms.

"He's just having a bad day. He didn't mean what he said."

Pessimists are the opposite. They discount good by saying it is temporary, non-personal, and specific. Negative events to the pessimist are personal, permanent and pervasive.

"It's just my luck. Get a little ahead and something always goes wrong."

To change from a pessimist to an optimist Dr. Seligman presents the process he calls Disputation. Using his ABCDE Model to change our explanatory style:

- We name the **Adversity**,
- Question our **Beliefs,**
- Analyze the **Consequences,**
- **Dispute** the inaccurate, and
- Become **Energized** through new insight and understanding.

To Dr. Seligman, optimism is not a Pollyanna-type glossing over of real problems. It is not naiveté. It is simply accepting life as inherently good and worthy of our concerted efforts. Work to adopt this outlook in your day-to-day life. Your optimistic attitude will have a profound impact on you, your staff, and your workplace.

The "No Moan" Zone

A large surgical eye center once had a problem with employee rivalry between divisions. Some employees constant negative attitudes severely dampened the morale of the entire office. I was called in to help reduce the tension and stress level in the practice. I came up with the "No Moan Zone," a declaration which was posted in the office break room. The owner was the first to sign it. Most other employees

Chapter 2 – No Moan Zone

 FYI! PDF's of these forms are available online at:
www.osteryoungobrien.com
enter code: **OST+OBR=2010**

<u>(Ex. The company break room)</u>
is hereby declared a

"No Moan Zone"

We, the undersigned members of
<u>(Your Company Name)</u>

agree to make this office a "No Moan Zone." We will not initiate, listen to, or participate in nonprofessional activities in word or deed toward this Company or other members of the staff, including:

Gossip, hearsay, back biting, ridicule, unwarranted criticism, complaining or undermining someone else's work.

We realize that every organization has problems as they grow. There are enough external challenges facing us and we do not need to add tension in this place of business to those challenges.

Each of us agrees to abide by the "No Moan Zone," even if others fail to do their part.
A fire cannot burn without fuel.

(Employees Signatures)

(Owner/Manager Signature)

signed it immediately. Several employees (the worst offenders) actually quit. At first, the owner thought, "What have I bought into?" They soon found that new employees who saw the "No Moan Zone" and had it explained, bought into the concept. Within a few months the office was a much happier place.

A "No Moan Zone" transformed this workplace. Others have used it successfully, too. If you have a problem with negative employees, this strategy could work for you as well.

Chapter Wrap-Up

Chapter Wrap-Up

In this chapter you have learned:

- The principles and practices of your employees become your corporate culture.

- Get employee opinions/feedback on what would make work more enjoyable.

- Use an incentive plan, when appropriate, to keep up employee morale.

- Only use an incentive plan that your employees can achieve.

- Let your employee have input into designing the incentive plan.

- A monetary gift should only be linked with an employee's productivity and/or performance, not a holiday.

- Change your work behavior from pessimism to optimism by using Dr. Seligman's ABCDE Model.

Chapter 2 – Corporate Culture

 PDF's of these forms are available online at:
www.osteryoungobrien.com
enter code: **OST+OBR=2010**

Evaluating Your Corporate Culture:

Is it difficult to raise concerns? If yes, then why? _____
_____
_____

Is bad behavior tolerated? If yes, then why? _____
_____
_____

If bad behavior has been tolerated until now, how will you correct this? _____
_____

What is your target date for correcting bad behaviors? _____

What problems might arise from the correction process? How will you handle them? _____
_____
_____

What are your goals for the business? _____
_____
_____

What are the employee's goals for the business? _____
_____
_____

Chapter 2 – Involving Staff

Are the goals of the employees the same as the owner's? If not how do they differ and how will you combine them into one common goal? _____
_____

Are ethical values supported and maintained? If not, why? How will you correct the problem? _____
_____

Do you have the tools and resources you need to be successful at your job? _____
_____

How would you describe this culture? _____
_____

Involving your Staff:

How do you plan to involve your employees in an effort to make work more enjoyable? _____
_____
_____

List your top five ideas for making work more enjoyable: _____
_____
_____

*List the top five ideas to make work more enjoyable presented by your employees:*_____
_____
_____

What dreams/expectations do you hold for your company? _____
_____

Chapter 2 – Incentive Systems

 PDF's of these forms are available online at:
www.osteryoungobrien.com
enter code: **OST+OBR=2010**

How can you share these dreams /expectations with your
employees? _____

_____

_____

What is your method for overcoming "Routine Boringness"?_____

_____

_____

Incentive Systems:

What areas in your business can you use for incentive purposes? ____

_____

_____

Do you feel more comfortable about giving monetary, time, or a
combination of the two, for employee incentives? Why? _____

_____

_____

Will your incentive plan interfere with the business' productivity
and/or profits? If so, is there a way to alter the plan so that is does
not? _____

_____

_____

Chapter 2 – Positive Leadership

Positive Leadership:

Do you consider yourself to be a pessimist or an optimist? _____
_____

Check which of the following you use to describe positive change:

❑ *Personal*	*or*	❑ *Non-personal*
❑ *Permanent*	*or*	❑ *Temporary*
❑ *Pervasive*	*or*	❑ *Specific*

If you checked more on the left column, you are considered a pessimist. If you checked more on the right column, you are considered an optimist.

According to the survey, are you a pessimist or an optimist? _____
_____

How can you use the information learned in the survey, along with Dr. Seligman's ABCDE Model, to reach your target goals with your business? _____
_____
_____
_____

 PDF's of these forms are available online at:
www.osteryoungobrien.com
enter code: **OST+OBR=2010**

Chapter 2 – Take-Aways & Action Steps

Take-Aways and Action Steps

1. _____
_____
Completion Date: _____
Results: _____
_____

2. _____
_____
Completion Date: _____
Results: _____
_____

3. _____
_____
Completion Date: _____
Results: _____
_____

4. _____
_____
Completion Date: _____
Results: _____
_____

5. _____
_____
Completion Date: _____
Results: _____
_____

Flatter me, and I may not believe you. Criticize me, and I may not like you. Ignore me, and I may not forgive you. Encourage me, and I will not forget you."

– William Arthur Ward

Chapter 3

Motivational Leadership

• •

Chapter At-A-Glance

By the end of this chapter you will know:

- How and why it is important to share trust between you and your employees.
- Your employees need to feel appreciated.
- How to show your appreciation to your employees.
- Why following through on your promises is important to gaining and maintaining employee trust.
- Why controlling your emotions and showing them when appropriate is important.
- Why you should be consistent in your expectations.

If you ask most employees why they quit their job, the answer would come down to one issue: TRUST. Trust is the ingredient that keeps employees happy. Trust is an implied agreement to live up to both parties' expectations. For a business owner, expectations of both customers and employees are very similar. By understanding the basic concepts of developing and helping to nurture trust, you can maintain and enhance your bottom line.

One of the first steps that leaders should take is to develop trust with their staff. The military teaches its soldiers to follow commands regardless of what they think. While a civilian leader certainly cannot expect to inspire this kind of blind obedience, a leader must develop something similar to the trust demanded by military leaders. More specifically, civilian employees should be willing, within reason, to do whatever their leader requests without doubting that the leader's path is the best.

When most leaders start overseeing employees, they do not have the trust of the staff - and this is normal. Staff are cordial, but naturally skeptical towards new bosses.

Trust is not automatic; it must be developed. A new leader earns trust by showing that he or she will look out for the organization and for all its team members.

Trust is a critical element in improving your relationship with your employees. As you work to increase trust in your business, both your work environment and your profits should improve.

■■ Inspect What You Expect ■■

Any great business owner should clearly articulate what the company's expectations are for its employees. While many businesses accomplish this important step, it is the process of inspecting what you expect that is so critical in ensuring expectations are successfully met. You cannot expect all employees to perform correctly all the time. They need to be inspected for two reasons:
1) To insure that a quality product is being delivered.
2) To let employees know that,

not only do you have high expectations, you will also insure they are met.

Inspecting what you expect will have a tremendous impact on your business by:
1) Showing the staff that you follow through consistently and regularly. As human beings, we all need a good dose of consistency in our lives.
2) Without inspections problems are discovered by accident often making it far too late to correct the problem. By inspecting what you expect, you can nip a problem in its

infancy, long before it becomes a major problem.

3) Inspections give your staff regular, accurate feedback.

This philosophy of inspecting what you expect is very inexpensive to administer, but high returns are realized from the point of implementation.

Appreciation

A fundamental need of employees is to feel appreciated! Employees need to feel appreciated for their work, for their customer-oriented attitude and for their empathy towards fellow staff members. When you express appreciation you make them feel whole and worthwhile. Appreciation is the key to keeping your employees working hard and positively representing your company.

Many business owners feel that they show and convey their appreciation to thier employees often; however, most employees do not feel as appreciated as their employers think they do. Why does this dichotomy exist? Because many entrepreneurs just say what they feel their employees want to hear, rather

Employee Appreciation

Here are 3 easy ways to show appreciation for your employees.

1. Take a staff member who has really made a significant contribution to lunch.
2. At staff meetings, tell the entire staff of the contributions of individual staff members.
3. Say, "Thank you." You cannot over estimate the importance of this. A "thank you" is just another good way to say, "I appreciate you," and it costs nothing.

Chapter 3 – Employee Appreciation

3 Types of Employee Appreciation

There are three types of appreciation all entrepreneurs should practice.

1. First, is the recognition that needs to be given when a specific task is done incredibly well.
2. The second type is appreciation of the associate himself/herself. Sometimes, it is good to walk up to your staff and say, "You know, I am so pleased that you are part of our team."
3. The third type of appreciation is in understanding that each employee has a life outside of work. The more interest and respect you have for each staff member's life outside of the work environment, the more they will appreciate you. Give an extra paid half- or full- day off as a reward. And, only ask for overtime hours when critical.

than understanding what their employees need to hear.

Now, obviously, you cannot go around continuously saying great things about all of your employees. Rather, try to observe employees who are doing good work and recognize them on the spot for their efforts, perseverance, contributions or attitude.

Employees definitely work because they get paid. However, properly timed praise and expressions of appreciation will do more to instill trust and job satisfaction than a raise.

Gallup once conducted a survey of employees and found that 65% of workers had not been praised or recognized for over a year. Another study showed that firms with owners and managers who expressed appreciation to their employees realized three times more return on equity and assets than those firms with non-appreciative bosses. So, not only is showing

Chapter 3 – Critical Points to Ponder

appreciation good for staff turnover, it improves your bottom line as well.

Here are some succinct ways to help managers (or anyone else) express appreciation to others.

First, try to ensure praise refers specifically to a particular situation or character trait. For example saying, "Joyce, what a great job you did on the report today," is not nearly as effective as saying, "Joyce you did a wonderful job on that report today. I can see how much time you spent on it. Your diligence and thoroughness are evident. I really appreciate your effort on the report. Thank you." Notice how this specificity communicates much more information and thankfulness.

> ## Critical Points to Ponder
>
> 1. **Understand the importance of listening and how to improve general communication skills for both you and your staff.**
>   a) Realize that communicating is at least a two-way street. Sometimes it is much more complex than that.
>   b) Work to align what you think, feel, say and do. Communicating involves much more than just words.
>   c) Listen then rephrase to insure that you understood.
>   d) Be specific, give details.
>   e) Good communication is defined as 75% listening and 25% talking.
>
> 2. **Situational Leadership allows you to enable employees.** Help employees think through any situation that causes them confusion or hesitation. Emphasize the systematic process you use. This will help them develop their own processes for future situations, and to deal with problems individually and independently in the future.

Chapter 3 – Appreciation

Another aspect to be aware of concerning praise is to ensure it is timely and sincere. Saying, "Joe, that was a great job on the expansion project two weeks ago," simply is not effective. It would be much better for a manager to say, "Joe, the report you submitted today was well written and well done. I really appreciate your effort on this. Thank you."

When you communicate praise, state the praise without commingling any other information. "Jessie, what a super job you did on the project that was due today. You're numerical analysis was excellent. Thank you. Oh, could you check on the status of the XYZ account?" Adding the last request for information dilutes the entire praise statement. Have praise be a standalone event.

The final element in communicating praise is to make sure you tell employees how their work impacts the entire firm. The more you can relate your praise to the team, the better. Stating, "Betty, you did a great job on the proposal you submitted to XYZ and it was accepted," is okay. However, it would be more concrete to say, "Betty, you did a great job on the proposal you submitted to XYZ. Because of your efforts, our team will be ranked as the best in the company. Congratulations and thank you!"

Praising your staff will make a tremendous difference to the financial well-being of your company and the morale of your staff.

Power Quote!

"Pretend that every single person you meet has a sign around his or her neck that says, 'Make me feel important.' Not only will you succeed in sales, you will succeed in life."

- Mary Kay Ash

Chapter 3 – Following Through

Following Through

Another way to build up the trust bank is to follow through on all promises made. Your associates rely on your promises as the leader. When you do not deliver, big withdrawals are made from your trust bank.

In business settings during apparent small talk, people often make statements and promises with little conscious thought and with no intention of following through. If the person receiving the message takes the other person at their word, and acts based on what they heard, it can lead to problems, disappointment or even animosity. This is especially true when the statement is made from someone higher up in the hierarchy to someone lower down.

The adage "Say what you mean and mean what you say" applies here. Almost all of us have pet sayings and sign-offs we use when we

> **Power Quote!**
>
> *"Does what you say and what you do match up? Be consistent!"*
> -Tim O'Brien

communicate. Try to become more conscious of what you say and when you say it. Being aware will help you be more precise and accurate in your speech.

If you say something, remember that you said it. Keep notes if needed. Then, deliver on what you promised.

Nothing destroys trust faster than being less-than-truthful with your staff. Being a leader demands that you develop trust. Being truthful, being a promise-keeper, being sensitive and being competent build trust. These good habits ensure the requisite amount of trust is there for you to lead.

Chapter 3 – Employee Trust

4 Steps To Employee Trust

1 **Do not blindside the other party.**
People, as a general rule, do not like surprises. For example, changing health insurance companies on employees without advance notice destroys trust. Keep an open communication loop whenever there is a chance that pending decisions can have a surprising or disruptive impact on your employees.

2 **Be consistent.**
Employees want to have a consistent level of treatment for all staff members. Treating certain employees differently (whether as favorites or as scapegoats) creates an inconsistent environment. Failing to be consistent across the board will destroy trust, and could possibly expose you to liability issues.

3 **Be there.**
If a problem develops for an employee, he wants you to be there. Of course, no one expects you to be in your office 24 hours a day, but when you get a call or e-mail you should follow up within one day.

4 **Exceed expectations.**
By far, exceeding expectations does more to improve trust than anything else does. Do not take this as saying, "Give your employees sizable raises." Rather, understand it as a recommendation that you give your employees more than what they are asking for on the job. Build up trust by giving them more resources and support than they have asked for to get their job done.

Emotions

Most of us have a knack for personalizing events that are beyond our control. The traffic light, directed by its timer, changes and we get mad, as if there were someone watching us approach saying, "OK, Harry, change the light, here she comes." We are curious creatures sometimes.

Examples like these usually make us laugh. And most of us could add many a personal favorite to the list. However, there is a darker side to personalizing events beyond our control. The problems occur when we allow our responses to become automatic, mindless habits. We display anger or frustration without conscious decision. An event occurs and we react.

For the next few days, play the role of witness. Watch how you respond to the various events of your life. What are these responses? Don't force emotions during this exercise. You may get angry, raise your voice, or lose your patience, but you don't have to. Just observe.

After noting your responses, decide which

◁ Leadership vs. Management ▷

Understand the difference between Leadership and Management. They require similar but different mental and emotional approaches.

- **Management**: deals with handling differences to maximize efficiency and productivity. It has an individual I/you/me focus.
- **Leadership**: focuses on vision and similarities. It strives to develop *esprit d'corp* and group cohesiveness. It has a group we/us focus.

Management and Leadership are both important. They often move in tandem. However, never confuse them as being identical.

Chapter 3 – Emotions Affect Employees

negative emotion you display the most. Is it depression and withdrawal? Is it anger or indifference? Work to defuse the emotion over time, altering the habit that causes the response. At first, you will catch yourself after the fact and say, "Oh, I did it again!" With practice, though, you will begin to catch yourself in the act and even "feel it coming on."

Each business owner and manager must remember that his or her emotions affect the morale of the entire organization. Showing emotions connotes trust: you must feel comfortable with another person to share your feelings. However, excessively strong emotions can make people wary of you. *Business owners should work to keep their emotions in balance – neither too high, nor too low.*

Emotions Affect Employees

One business owner had a hard time controlling his temper. He was easily angered. As a result, his staff avoided him at all cost. They were reluctant to share any information with him for fear he would level his temper at them. His employees felt no loyalty to the business or its owner, and many were seeking other jobs.

A second business owner showed no feelings at all. When things were going well, she did not express any satisfaction. As a result, her staff was frustrated, feeling as though they could never live up to her expectations or make her happy.

A third business owner expressed all his feelings to the extreme. When he was happy and excited, the whole office felt it. However, when he was down, it was so awful that the up times could not make up for it. As a result, the staff felt as if they were riding on a giant yo-yo! They knew they could not get too excited when their boss was happy because, at any moment, his mood might change.

Chapter 3 – Consistency

Consistency

As our world has become more and more complicated, managers must deliver consistency in their management style or risk losing their staff's confidence. While our favorite fast-food hamburgers might be pretty cruddy, they are consistently cruddy so we continue trade off having a good hamburger for one that is consistent. Why is this? We as human beings need consistency in our lives in order to cope with a very complex and dynamic world.

Consistency and expectation go hand-in-hand. Most employees working in your business want to know how you will react in given situations. It is better to have a standard response every time a given issue or event occurs than to respond erratically. Consistency is an important part of every business.

When dealing with employees, strive to achieve the highest quality of feedback and support you can while maintaining consistency. The trade off of higher quality for lower consistency is just not worth the sacrifice. You cannot treat one employee well and another poorly. You cannot have favorites or scapegoats. As a leader, you must strive to be consistent in your interactions

Chapter 3 – Don't Loose Employee Trust

with every employee. An inconsistent leader will not develop trust, and employees will not follow leaders they do not trust.

Develop a short "cheat sheet" and carry it with you, as a reminder. (There are examples included at the end of this chapter.) On the cheat sheet list: "The top 5 Qualities I most admire in a great employee,"

"The 5 'Poison Actions' that I cannot tolerate in my business," and "The top 5 New Goals I have for my company." Then at every appropriate opportunity, praise the Top 5 Qualities in public. Express your concerns about the 5 Poisons in private, and remind everyone of the company's current goals. That will help you remain consistent.

Don't Lose Employee Trust

Employees need to be able to trust you, or your credibility goes out the window.

- A firm had some cash flow problems, so they unilaterally cut the sales staff salaries and commissions in order to balance the budget. You guessed it: they lost every single salesperson – the staff no longer trusted their management.

- Another business owner decided she needed to improve profitability and, without notice, eliminated the coffee and coffee makers she had been providing for over five years. Obviously, the staff felt as if they had been blindsided, and the morale of the organization plummeted.

Leaders and managers are only effective if employees feel they can trust them.

If this is not the case, the employee will simply be unable and unwilling to trust the manager.

The employee will either begin seeking another job, or will reduce his or her work output to the absolute minimum.

Chapter Wrap-Up

Chapter Wrap-Up

In this chapter you have learned:

- One of the first things a leader should do is develop trust between themselves and their employees.
- Most employees quit their job because they feel under appreciated.
- Show your appreciation for your employees by saying *"Thank you,"* and *"I appreciate you and your hard work."*
- Three types of appreciation all entrepreneurs should practice are:
  - **1)** Give recognition for a task that is done exceptionally well.
  - **2)** Appreciation expressed to each specific employee for the opportunity to work with them. ★
  - **3)** *Understand and acknowledge that the employee has a life outside of the work environment. Respect their personal time.*
- The 4 Steps to Employee Trust are :
  - **1)** Don't blindside others.
  - **2)** Be consistent.
  - **3)** Be there.
  - **4)** Exceed expectations.
- QTIP = **Q**uit **T**aking **I**t **P**ersonally.
  - Don't get mad at things out of your control.
- Your emotions affect the morale of your entire staff.
- Consistency is an important part of every successful business. Don't pick favorites or scapegoats amongst your employees.

Top 5 Qualities

**Use this form to write out the top five
qualities you admire most in a great employee.**

Quality # 1 _____

Quality # 2 _____

Quality # 3 _____

Quality # 4 _____

Quality # 5 _____

Which of your employees show theses qualities? _____
_____
_____

*When given the opportunity, how will you express your
appreciation to that employee?* _____
_____
_____

*If none of your employees has these qualities, how will you fix the
situation?* _____
_____
_____

Top 5 Poison Actions

Use this form to write out the top five Poison Actions that you cannot tolerate from an employee.

Action # 1 _____

Action # 2 _____

Action # 3 _____

Action # 4 _____

Action # 5 _____

Are any of your current employees expressing any of these actions? _____
_____

If yes, who is/are the trouble employee(s)? _____
_____

What steps will you take to correct the problem(s)? _____
_____
_____

FYI! PDF's of these forms are available online at:
www.osteryoungobrien.com
enter code: **OST+OBR=2010**

Top 5 Company Goals

Use this form to write out the top five new company goals you would like to achieve. When and how will you measure success?

Goal # 1 _____

Goal # 2 _____

Goal # 3 _____

Goal # 4 _____

Goal # 5 _____

How/when will you achieve Goal #1? _____
_____

How/when will you achieve Goal #2? _____
_____

How/when will you achieve Goal #3? _____
_____

How/when will you achieve Goal #4? _____
_____

How/when will you achieve Goal #5? _____
_____

Chapter 4

Mentoring & Coaching

Chapter At-A-Glance

In this chapter you will learn:

- The importance of seeing the hidden potential in your employees.

- The difference between a Mentor and a Coach.

- How to choose a mentor.

- How often/if you should use a coach.

- The three biggest obstacles preventing your staff from performing their best.

One of the biggest mistakes employees and managers make is failing to see every staff member's potential. It is easy to form beliefs about your staff solely on the basis of past behavior rather than recognizing the unique potential that each one brings daily to the workforce. For example, if a staff member constantly makes mistakes on a certain type of report, many managers would define the employee in terms of those errors rather than seeing their unbridled potential.

Jim Moran, the founder of the Jim Moran Family Enterprises and Southeast Toyota, was very successful in the automotive industry. Without exception, he made his staff feel great. This was not

Chapter 4 - Mentoring vs. Coaching

Mentoring vs. Coaching

Coach? Mentor? What's the difference?

Sometimes people use the words coach and mentor interchangeably. Admittedly, there are times when the roles merge and overlap - however, coaches and mentors usually serve in distinctly different roles.

- Mentors focus on life improvement and value development.

- The mentored usually sets the pace and contacts the mentor when he has questions or feels he needs guidance and/ or support.

- A mentor usually assumes the role for free.

- A mentor can become a coach when the mentored needs specific instruction and guidance on a new skill set.

- Mentoring often lasts for years allowing a bond of mutual respect and even caring to develop between the mentor and the mentored.

- Coaches concern themselves with specific performance improvement.

- Coaches are normally "in charge," of those they coach and set the schedule.

- Coaches are normally compensated.

- When their coaching time with an individual is over, coaches often become mentors to that same person.

- Coaching lasts for a limited duration (like a sports season), and the relationships between a coach and those coached is not one of equals.

just because he always had kind words for everyone, but rather because those around him sensed that he saw their real potential. It was like having a sudden gust of wind lift you up. He was loved and cherished by so many because he made them feel good simply by noticing their hidden potential.

Many managers try to coach their employees; however, the tendency is to change an employee's behavior on a given task. For instance, if a coaching session focuses only on the problems an associate had in his last report, the discussion gets bogged down in details. However, if you can encourage them to see their own potential for greatness, you are coaching to the potential, and the details will often get resolved as a result.

As a manager, you can draw much more out of your employees if you can visualize each one's inherent potential. Imagine a baseball manager

Seeing Potential

Be careful about your preconceptions. They can hold you back from seeing the potential in an employee. If you prejudge you stand the chance of missing some very positive surprises your employees have in store for you if given the opportunity to develop.

If you need new skill sets in your organization, look first for volunteers within your current staff. Maybe someone already knows how to do what you want done.

Look for aptitude. Has anyone in your group ever displayed or shown flashes of competence in a needed area?

Be fair and give people a chance to grow. However, don't expect brilliance over night.

trying to coach a hitter who has not had a hit in ten appearances at bat. The manager could coach the player to practice more, or he could tell the player to be patient and wait until the slump eventually ends.

However, a great manager would convey the potential that he knows is within his player, and help him to see this as well.

You should frequently stop and take note of the greatness in all of your support staff. If you do not, you run the risk of seeing them as obstacles. Seeing the potential of each person you work with allows you to have a very special relationship with each one. As a coach, you need to note their greatness and show them how they can see it, too. Somehow it is much easier for others to see our potential than it is for us to see our own.

Now do the best you can to see the potential in each and every one of your staff members!

Mentoring

Employees need advice and a chance to vent their problems. Without a guide, it can be very difficult to work though issues or questions that come up in the workplace. Often employees will come to the business owner only as a last resort. As a result, issues may be dragged out, becoming next to impossible to solve.

An effective way to address this problem is by assigning a mentor to each worker. It is the mentor's job to make the employee feel at home in the company and to be a sounding board. As most mentors have been with the

Power Tip!

Some of the typical problems that mentors can help solve include:

- How to deal with a problem employee.
- How to improve the morale in the organization.
- How to establish an incentive system.

company longer than the one mentored, they are usually capable of giving wise advice about the inner workings of

Chapter 4 - Choosing a Mentor

Choosing a Mentor

When thinking about which employees would make good mentors, keep in mind what characteristics they will need.

- First and foremost, a mentor should be a good listener. Poor listeners cannot hear the entire problem.

- Secondly, a mentor should have some experience in the same field as the employee they will mentor.

- Since any question is fair game, the candidates for mentor must be comfortable with a wide variety of issues.

- Finally, they should be someone with whom the mentored can feel very secure about telling whatever is on their mind.

the company, including how to maximize one's potential for promotion. Mentoring costs little, but pays high dividends.

Mentoring provides an employee the opportunity to work with a successful senior employee whose focus is developing and guiding the newer employee. In most mentorship programs, there is no fee involved; the mentor just enjoys the chance to help another employee.

One way to cultivate mentoring in your business is to encourage your employees to pay attention to people they admire and respect, and ask them to be their mentor. In this scenario, the mentor does not necessarily need to be another employee of your company. In other cases, you may want to ask senior employees in your business to mentor specific individuals and work to develop their careers. Most people feel honored when asked to be a mentor.

Mentors should meet with their mentees for at least one hour every two weeks. Encourage your employees to have three to four very specific questions written down for

> ### Profitable Secrets
>
> Empirical data clearly shows that mentoring leads to improved profitability. A mentor's knowledge and skills add significant value, and all it takes to get one is having the courage to ask someone. Most people are honored to be a mentor. Work to develop a mentoring network with and for your staff.

that meeting and to stick to the agenda. Have your employees send a list of questions to their mentor beforehand to make this time together more productive.

Coaching

The Oxford Dictionary defines coaching as, "the verb to tutor, train, give hints to, prime with facts." Socrates talked about coaching more than 2,400 years ago. He defined it as, "unlocking the person's potential."

Coaching should be conducted on a regular basis to help each staff member reach their potential. A great manager spends the majority of her time doing this. Coaching is useful both in addressing specific performance issues and as an ongoing part of developing an employee's potential. Always be on the look-out for opportunities to coach. Be careful though, it can be overdone. By adapting the approach to each employee, the sensitive manager will know when to push forward and when to hold back.

The secret of coaching is to look at potential not performance. The key is to not limit a worker by his or her last performance, but instead to look ahead to what could possibly be done at the next similar opportunity. While performance is important (we have performance reviews and goals for a reason), potential is the key to growth and new ideas. Managers must train themselves to think of each employee in terms of his or her potential and not just in terms of their current performance.

The biggest road blocks to reaching potential are: fear of failure, lack of confidence in the company or its plans, and self-doubt that they have what it takes to succeed. As a coach you must counter these negative thoughts and set your employees at ease. Some associates will present bigger coaching challenges than others. Just remember, if you believe that an employee is valuable to the company and that he fits into the company's long term plans, then he is worth the effort to coach. Persevere!

Coaching Key Points

- Ask the right questions.

- Be specific and sufficiently detailed.

- Listen thoroughly with eye contact.

- Try to understand if fear is driving the staff. If it is, find ways to effectively deal with it.

- Understand the value of coaching and mentoring and use each appropriately.

- Recognize that you should coach and/or mentor all of your staff. Have it be an on-going part of your company culture.

Coaching Awareness

Outside awareness and self-awareness are crucial for coaching. Outside awareness is knowing what is happening around you, while self-awareness is knowing what you are experiencing inside as a result of what is happening around you. Outside awareness calls for a keen sense of perception, and observation. Self-awareness deals with perceiving the impact of your surroundings on your attitudes, feelings and assessments of your environment.

An effective coach strives to develop outside awareness and self-awareness in those they coach. Once a person develops these qualities to a functional degree, they become much more self-sufficient and coachable.

Coaching Tools

A simple heuristic to help you when coaching others is:

P+A=R
Perception plus Attitude equals Response

If you're not getting the responses you want or need, check the perceptions (beliefs) and attitudes of both you and those you coach.

Another, similar way to look at human activity is to view it as a continuous series of *Inputs, Processes and Outputs*.

The *inputs* are our perceptions.

The *processes* are all of the preconceptions, opinions and attitudes we assign to those inputs based on our beliefs and past experiences.

The *outputs* are our actions or reactions to the inputs.

These are two tools you can use to assist you in your coaching adventures.

■Responsibility & Questions■

As a coach you must personally exhibit and teach responsibility to those you coach. Choice is a critical factor in allowing responsibility to have some impact. Without choices, alternatives and options, it is difficult to encourage associates to take an active role in problem solving.

Ask questions. Asking questions, and discussing the answers leads the staff to take responsibility for the issue at hand. Questions allow open dialog, while statements close down conversation. Proper questions increase both awareness and responsibility and allow each worker to both contribute input and assume some measure of responsibility. Give the employee the opportunity to actively participate in both the discovery and recovery processes.

> **Questions**
>
> Questions have to start broadly and then narrow down with more specific information. You do not want to start with,
>
> *"Why did you screw up that customer's order so badly?"*
>
> Rather,
>
> *"How have your last couple of weeks at work been?"*
>
> Leading questions are manipulative. Instead of
>
> *"Have you considered (insert suggestion)?"*
>
> It would be better to say,
>
> *"What other options would help you here?"*

Listening

A good coach listens more than he talks and does so without interrupting. Take notes, make eye contact, nod your head in agreement and discuss what you've heard after the individual you are coaching has stopped sharing.

Listening is critically important to coaching. Talking either too much or at the wrong time is counter-productive to effective coaching. You can not help the individual you are coaching unless you know the issues; you can learn nothing while talking. Active listening will not only allow you to obtain a more complete and accurate understanding, but will also convey a sense of warmth and value.

After you are done listening, summarize and reflect back to the employee, what you just heard. "I understood you to say that you feel you have too much work and not enough team assistance on your current project - is that correct?" This allows the employee to clarify

Listening Exercise

If you and/or your staff are not good listeners, it is a good idea to conduct listening exercises.

You can do this by having someone give a short, prepared statement that has 10 critical ideas or thoughts imbedded in it. Then, each person who listened is asked to give the top 10 points covered. Everyone's score is how many of the 10 imbedded ideas they recalled.

Another way to do this is by watching a video segment then discussing it and going back and rewatch it to see how closely the discussion aligned with the actual video.

Reward those who "get them all right," and emphasize to everyone how important it is to be an excellent listener.

any misperceptions you might have and shows the employee you have heard her correctly.

Your tone of voice is important, too. When it is your turn to talk, use a calm, reassuring tone of voice. Be serious if necessary, but take care not to speak too quickly or sharply. Speak confidently with no insinuation of threat in your tone. Remember a solution is your goal.

Coaching Problems

Anyone who has coached knows, and those who haven't will find, coaching is not a one-way ride of continuous positive experiences. Ideally, the majority of coaching experiences are positive and forward looking. However, there are those times when an employee's actions

Take-Home Points

- Coaching must be an ongoing process. It is not a "one-shot deal." Be tactful and perceptive of when to coach and when to back off, this will make you a more effective and likeable coach.

- Coaching is seeing the full potential in each and every employee no matter what his current performance is.

- Coaching is raising the awareness of each employee as it relates to a situation and having each staff member take responsibility through their correct choices.

- Coaching is asking questions that allow a staff member to discern the problem and participate in its solution.

- Listening is more important than talking. As the old adage goes, "God gave us two ears and one mouth so we should listen twice as much as we talk." ☺

Chapter 4 - Don't Be An Ostrich

require training in another direction. At this point, coaching should progress from initially encouraging and supporting the needed change, to clearly defined direction, to specific requirements and, finally, to termination if required. Handle problems with sensitivity and patience. Use your listening skills to ensure you understand the problem fully. Also, document every step of the discovery, consultation and resolution process. If you end up terminating the employee, you want to have the documentation on hand to show you handled the situation ethically and legally.

Let's examine some situations where we might apply the above principles.

> **Don't be an Ostrich**
>
> When you have problems, handle them head on. This does not mean you should act aggressively or combatively. It does mean you must acknowledge the problem exists.
>
> Accept that problems generally won't go away without action. Assess the problem, work toward an equitable solution, and then take steps to ensure the same problem doesn't occur again.

1. Habitual tardiness can throw the entire company off its schedule. If one employee is allowed to be tardy regularly it will either instill resentment or copy-cat behavior in others, neither of which is satisfactory. Post and distribute specific attendance policies clearly delineating the expectations for timeliness and the consequences of tardiness. Obviously some discretion is both kind and helpful, but that doesn't mean allowing an employee to take advantage of company kindness. Have all employees sign a form stating that they understand the attendance policies and that there is nothing that prevents

them from being on time regularly. Privately talk with any habitually tardy employees. Listen to their explanation. Ask if they understand the company policy. Ask for their solution to the current tardiness situation. If their solution is reasonable, ask if they will abide by it. If their solution is not reasonable or too vague, work to arrive at a mutual understanding. If there is flexibility in work hours, offer a different starting time in return for either a later stopping time or reduced compensation. After the meeting, send the employee a letter covering the points of agreement. If the situation continues, speak with them again. Remind them that their tardiness impacts the entire company and could be cause for termination, since it violates a known company policy.

2. Sometimes employees become anxious or curious about their future. Dealing with this situation depends on the employee's tenure, performance and the company's future plans. If the employee is fearful of losing a job and you can give them assurances, do so, without being too concrete or specific. If you either don't know what the future plan is or you know that the employee might not fit into a known

Termination

Sometimes termination is the only functional solution to an employee situation.

After you've exhausted all options and means, after you've made sure you have followed company guidelines and policies, after you've consulted with your attorney, and you know that there are no other options left but termination, set a date and time to terminate the employee.

future plan, then tactfully avoid a direct answer. Unfortunately, uncertainty is part of the fabric of business making it difficult to alleviate all the concerns an employee might have.

3. When an employee believes they have been unfairly passed over for promotion, be sure you know the facts from the company's perspective before you discuss it with the employee. You could speak to the difficulty of deciding between him and the candidate chosen. If you can offer specific suggestions for improving or developing missing skill sets, use the discussion with the employee as a coaching opportunity.

4. If you have a staff member who tries to control other employees there are several ways to view and approach this. The employee who wants to exert control, might have a legitimate argument about the others.

Maybe they aren't working hard enough. Maybe they aren't focused and drift off task making work more difficult for the controller. However, the employee might also hold the wrong position or have too much responsibility. Of course, it could simply be the personality of the controller, to. First, assess the situation for the underlying causes of the problem, then tailor your response to that assessment. Just telling

The coach's mirror

If you coach others, place this little saying on your bathroom mirror so you will see it every day.

"You are the only one I can't deceive when I say I've done my best and haven't."

Self honesty is often the solution to many situations.

someone to back off without knowing why she wants to exert control will not solve the situation.

Chapter Wrap-Up

Chapter Wrap-Up

In this chapter you have learned:

- You need to recognize each employee's potential not just the faults, and help each one to see his or her potential as clearly as you do.

- How to tell the difference between a Mentor and a Coach.

- What qualities a great Mentor should have.

- How to choose a Mentor for your newer employees.

- Coaching should be conducted on a regular basis to help staff members reach their potential.

- Three of the biggest obstacles to increased staff potential are: 1) Fear of Failure, 2) Lack of Confidence, and 3) Self Doubt.

- Outside Awareness and Self-Awareness are crucial for coaching.

- Listening is a critical aspect part of coaching.

Chapter 4 – Choosing & Pairing Mentors

 PDF's of these forms are available online at:
www.osteryoungobrien.com
enter code: **OST+OBR=2010**

Choosing and Pairing Mentors

Having mentors that newer employees feel comfortable with is very important. Make a list of the veteran employees who would work well as mentors and match them to your newer employees. While choosing mentors and pairing employees remember the following questions:

Do the mentor and the newer employee you've paired have experience in the same field? _____

Are the employees you selected to be mentors good listeners? _____

Are the employees you selected to be mentors trustworthy with personal information? _____

Mentor	Newer Employee
_____	_____
_____	_____
_____	_____
_____	_____
_____	_____
_____	_____

Chapter 4 – Mentor or Coach?

Are you a Mentor or a Coach?

Find out if you are considered a mentor or a coach to a specific person by answering the questions below. Whichever set you most frequently answer, "Yes," to is the role you play with that person.

Mentoring

Are you helping with life improvement and/or value development? _____

*Do you wait for the person to contact you with a problem?*_____

Do you volunteer your services/advice for free? _____

Does your service/advice last for years at a time? _____

Coaching

*Are you helping with a very specific performance improvement issue?*_____

*Do you seek out people to help and then take charge when you find someone to help?*_____

Do you charge for your services/advice? _____

Does your service/advice only last for a predetermined length of time? _____

Chapter 4 – Take Aways & Action Steps

Take-Aways and Action Steps

1. _____

_____

Completion Date: _____

Results:_____

_____

2. _____

_____

Completion Date: _____

Results:_____

_____

3. _____

_____

Completion Date: _____

Results:_____

_____

4. _____

_____

Completion Date: _____

Results:_____

_____

5. _____

_____

Completion Date: _____

Results:_____

_____

"One of the fastest ways to go out of business is to think you can do it all yourself."

-Tim O'Brien

Chapter 5

Training
• • • • • • • • • • • • • • • • •

Chapter At-A-Glance

By the end of this chapter you will know:
- How to conduct a productive and an effective seminar.
- How to give proper on-the-job-training to your employees.
- Why it is a good idea to cross-train your employees.
- The importance of a stand-in.
- If your employees really need training.
- How learning differs from being trained.

People learn better, and remember longer, when engaged in "spaced-interval learning." Situations like a weekend seminar where we experience "massed learning" chunks, or the "cramming" we may attempt the night before an exam, are rarely effective. Our minds absorb more when we take in smaller amounts of information in more frequent doses. For instance, five one-hour sessions separated by completely different activities, are more effective than a five-hour marathon session. This approach allows our minds time to absorb the information. Moderation and consistency, over time, equal significant productivity.

Seminars

Seminars are one of the most common methods to train and educate employees. While the speaker may be a hired professional, it is also common for the presentation to be given by a superior or another employee. Whether you choose to present the information yourself or delegate the task to another, here are some guidelines to help you make your point effectively and help your employees get the most out of the training.

1. Visual information has the greatest and longest-lasting impact. Show at least as much as you tell. Use pictures, color, diagrams, models, and even people to act out key concepts.

2. Be creative in making your point. Use multiple media. Bring in props, use music or whatever else would make the concepts memorable. Of course also be safe, practical, and appropriate.

3. Use multiple approaches to explain all your major points of focus. Strive for ways to present information with visual, auditory, and tactile stimuli. This ensures you hit all the major learning styles.

4. Lead your audience to the obvious conclusion by building up point-by-point. This way they will arrive at your planned information destination.

5. Use spaced-interval learning on major points. Reshow important visuals, repeat major points and ideas several times during your presentation. Put them in your summary, too.

Power Tip!

After your presentation is over, write out a few notes with details of what worked, what didn't work, and why. This will help you plan future presentations.

6. Use timing, silence, and "the pregnant pause" to increase your impact. Consider how comedians and serious actors use these devices. Ask questions, then wait for the answers. Lead, tease, and make them wait.

7. Interact with your audience where practical and not disruptive. Draw them into your presentation. Play games with them. Ask questions and make them answer.

8. Once you have taught a major lesson, reinforce the information by having participants role play. Set up a scenario that allows them to act out the lesson. Be sure to monitor the role playing to insure the correct transfer of knowledge. You don't want participants to start off with bad habits or an inaccurate interpretation.

9. Always maintain control. If you see people nodding off or talking to others, stop and have everyone stand and stretch. Before you begin, require everyone to turn off his or her cell phone or PDA.

10. If you make a mistake, admit it, smile, and move on. Do not allow it to disrupt you.

Seminar Tips

- Create visual impact
- Make your points in a creative way
- Be logical
- Use repetition
- Remember your timing
- Be interactive with the audience
- Maintain control
- Admit mistakes
- Keep moving

On-The-Job-Training

Employees who are learning skills they'll need on the job should learn in surroundings and situations that are as lifelike and natural as possible. Where and how the associates practice needs to be as close to the actual workplace as you can make it. When troops prepare for combat, part of their training involves live fire, (i.e., real bullets). Soldiers must know that their training is as real and potentially fatal as actual combat or they wouldn't learn those skills they need to survive.

When people practice in isolation or under conditions very different from what they can expect to find during the actual experience, it is an inferior type of practice. Instead, training should take place at regular intervals in short periods under actual conditions. Using this method, employees will learn better and remember the concepts longer.

Cross-Training

It is very common for a business owner to be "held hostage" by an employee. All employees are valuable, but you never want any employee to become invaluable. The minute an employee becomes indispensable, you become a victim. Sure, you want to keep great employees, but a productive, hard worker is very different from an employee who is becoming indispensable. It is not good business to become too reliant on one employee, if something happens to incapacitate that employee, it could become a crisis for you.

To keep this from happening, *it is important to cross-train other employees to perform a critical employee's job.* This cross-training

Chapter 5 – Cross-Training

1) Admit that your employees can't be experts on every subject, all the time. Work to give them an overview knowledge of many aspects of the business. Do not expect them to become expert in more than one or two fields.

2) Encourage your employees to willingly accept information from someone younger than or very familiar to them. Ideas and information can and do come from everywhere and everyone. Foster an open, receptive, and responsive environment for all avenues of experience and information.

3) When meeting with employees, list areas where they desire to improve. Set goals with them for improving the top three or four. Review and revise this list as they grow and become more proficient.

4) Stay focused on the benefits of success in a given area. If the task is a better understanding of technology, have an employee learn one program at a time, then implement what was learned. If an associate's goal is a raise or a better job in the organization, help her learn new skills or perfect current ones to attain it.

should include making it the employee's job to train a subordinate to be his or her replacement. Succession, or replacement, planning should be mandatory in every organization. This must be put into effect, not just for the business owner, but also for every critical employee.

Cross-training is the systematic process used to train workers to do their associates' jobs. Ideally, cross-training should be done both vertically and horizontally. Managers need to cross-train into jobs of other managers as well as into lower-level jobs.

Cross-training needs

Chapter 5 - Cross-Training

to be carefully planned, and embraced by all your workers. Throwing someone into a new job when another employee is absent can create chaos. Understanding this will help your associates to buy into the effort of cross-training. Once you educate them about the benefits, request their assistance in planning the process. The more employee input you have, the better.

The idea of a yearly master plan that spells out who is going to be cross-trained and when, gives employees plenty of time to prepare for this adventure.

There are many benefits to cross-training, including giving employees more variety in their work.

Power Quote!

"Cross-training is like having a spare tire. It is risky and unsafe to embark on a trip without a spare tire. Likewise, the risks are too great to run a company without cross-training."
    - Jerry Osteryoung

Power Tip!

Have a plan for cross-training AND follow through with it. A plan can't take another employee's place.

Cross-train everyone so no single employee can hold you back or hold the company hostage.

Do not allow an employee to avoid being cross-trained. Everyone must cross-train or you'll have a potentially fatal flaw in your plan.

The more variety a job has, the happier the employee. Cross-training improves teamwork, as employees becomes more aware of what their coworkers do. It also allows each associate to understand what he needs to do to make work flow more smoothly in the department.

Cross-training often erases differences and unhealthy competition. Once workers understand what others jobs entail, they tend to develop more empathy for their coworkers. Often you hear, "I had no idea that their job was so difficult!" Walking in the shoes of another person has the potential to develop compassion for the person and allow artificial barriers to fall.

Cross-training can also be an alarm bell for complacent or lethargic employees. Moving the employees (on a temporary basis) under the aegis of cross-training usually results in the employee's coming back with increased motivation.

Stand-ins

This section deals with having employees trained to temporarily take over in the absence of the owner or other major employee. There are many names for this person: substitute, proxy, replacement, surrogate or stand-in are a few.

The first rule of business is to implement a plan for grooming others to take over for you or your key employees when you and/or they are away. It is recommended that every business owner or key manager train one employee to make decisions up to a certain amount of risk or dollars. If you have no one in your business to fill in for you, then you need to groom or hire someone for this.

Another reason for having a "stand-in boss" strategy is that it makes your

> **Power Tip!**
>
> - Identify talent early that have great potential.
> - Develop a plan for grooming your staff to reach the next level.
> - Find a coach or mentor for each of these talented staff members.
> - Set up a regular feedback loop to measure progress.

business more valuable when you need or want to sell it. Most buyers want the assurance that there will be a smooth transition when the seller departs. Nothing facilitates this better than having someone groomed to take over in your

Chapter 5 – Why Have a Stand-in?

Why Have A Stand-in?

"I once wrote a little bit about my vacation at a Dude Ranch in Colorado and the travails with my horse Sunshine. One of the neater horseback excursions began at 5:30 a.m., when we rolled out of bed, saddled our horses, and rode up into the Rockies, one of the most beautiful parts of the world. We were treated to majestic mountain views from all vantage points and a wonderful breakfast in the mountains prepared by the wranglers. There was only one problem."

"Cell phones will not work on the ranch as it is in a valley; however, when you get up higher, the darn things start to work. On this peaceful breakfast ride, an entrepreneur from Orlando spent the entire time (yes, even on the back of her horse) conducting business. She destroyed her vacation because she had no one back home to make decisions. She also impacted everyone else's vacation with this intrusion into their serenity. (I fault the owner of the dude ranch. They should have a no cell phone policy on their ranch that everyone signs before arriving.)"

"Obviously, this entrepreneur with the cell phone branded to her ear had no one she felt comfortable with making decisions in her absence. Her vacation (mine too) would have been so much more enjoyable if the strategic planning for her business had included empowering an employee to make critical decisions in her absence."

-Jerry Osteryoung

absence. If your operation can run without you, you have a business. If you are indispensable you simply have an ongoing promotion that is tied to you.

There will be (and should be) times when you need to get away knowing that everything will be running smoothly when you return. If you do not have this confidence, then you need to develop a strategy for finding a competent stand-in to act on your behalf. Also, once you have identified a stand-in, let them act without interruption. You and you representative will both be better off if you do. Another key ingredient in the formula for an effective stand-in is empowerment. The substitute and those they will direct must know without a doubt, that the stand-in is actually you when you are away and has the power to make and carry out key decisions.

Power Tip for Sole Proprietor!

If you are a "one-person show," or have few employees, the suggestions and ideas in this book are also for you.

For example: if you have no one who can stand in for you, block out the same vacation time each year, preferably during your slowest times, and simply close down during that time. Let everyone know well in advance. Leave emergency numbers and check e-mail or voice mail once per day but do your best to not let others high-jack your vacation. Remember, you DO NEED time off.

▬ To Train or Not to Train? ▬

That really IS the question!

Training is NOT always the answer. That might sound like an odd line for a chapter on training, however it is true.

Very often, when a problem or challenge arises in a department or across an organization, the first impulse is to throw training at it. The logic runs along the following lines: "There is a problem, it must be because our people aren't trained properly. What else could it possibly be?"

The reality is training is often the most expensive answer to a problem. You

Chapter 5 – To Train or Not to Train

should consider everything else before declaring training to be the solution. So again you ask, "What else could it be?"

If you have a technology problem, the cause might be slow computers, ineffective software, or inadequate capacity. The solution here often is more or different technology, not training. While the costs of fixing it might be even more expensive than training, training will not solve a problem caused by technological deficiencies.

Maybe morale is the issue. This can be caused by inadequate lighting, a dull work environment or a single poison employee. You fix this with full spectrum lights, a new paint job and either a transferred, transformed, or released team member.

Communications might be problematic. Potential causes could be an inconsistent company policy, a manager who shows favoritism, intra-department rivalries and inter-department competition. Company policy changes and

> **Power Quote!**
>
> *"Certainly, finding the root cause of any problem is much more important than coming up with a glib solution."*
> - Jerry Osteryoung

clear impartial guidance will solve these problems.

Before you decide on training, be certain that it is the only and best solution. Assess the situation first. Then analyze where you actually are compared to your ideal situation. Any difference between your ideal and the present situation is the performance gap you must fill.

Once you are cognizant of your gap, list all the ways you can think of to close or minimize it. First, think outside the training box. If, in the end, training is the correct solution, it should be obvious. Then, get training where indicated and make sure it actually addresses the problem. Non-targeted training is very expensive

Learning vs. Training

One thing every business needs to work on is upgrading the skills of their staff. This is critical for several reasons. New technologies are constantly emerging, people are promoted or are given new responsibilities, and existing skills need to be reinforced and refined.

Most businesses these days talk about training, with many having entire departments dedicated to training their workers. However, this emphasis is misplaced. Rather, the focus should be on learning. Indeed many larger companies are now changing their training departments to learning departments. While this might just seem like a subtle change in wording, it is actually much bigger.

Most training programs, emphasize the trainer who disseminates information to participants. It is the trainer's

Key Differences

Training	Learning
1. Training is instructor-centered.	1. Learning is student-centered.
2. Managers encourage and provide tools.	2. Learners accept responsibility for mastering the material.
3. Training is often a single seminar or presentation.	3. Learning is an ongoing process until mastery is achieved.
4. Trainers are often hired to conduct a presentation, and then leave the work environment.	4. Learning requires metrics to measure progress.
	5. Managers make sure the learning translates to the work environment for the good of the company.

responsibility to convey information. Training is simply an event staff members attend. Learning, on the other hand, is an internal event. It transfers the responsibility to the participant. It is now up to each learner to understand and master the material. Between training and learning, the focus shifts from teacher to student.

When conducting a seminar tell the participants you are not there to train them; rather, you are there to facilitate their learning process. The outcome of this seminar rests on their learning the necessary material. It is their responsibility to master the material, and not yours to train them. This is a big shift in orientation, but it is one that is vital in business.

This new philosophy requires that each participant comes into the learning environment with a clear understanding that the responsibility for mastering the material is his or hers and not the instructor's. In addition, the manager plays a key role in ensuring that the learning is transferred into the employee's work environment. The manager is responsible for providing the encouragement, tools and support that will enable the employee to successfully apply the new

Reward Progress

Learning can and should be fun, however, the road to mastering new skills can be bumpy.

1) As a manager or employer, set up benchmarks along the way to new skills for your employees, and regularly monitor their progress.

2) Acknowledge that the material can be difficult.

3) Give praise along the way and celebrate success.

Let your people know that they are important, and that what they are doing is important to the company. Tell them you are proud of them for their newly acquired skill sets.

skills and knowledge to his or her day-to-day activities.

Some people might say that the distinction between learning and training is minor, but it actually changes the entire way we approach new material. Learning, begins at a higher motivation point, allowing students to become active participants in the process as opposed to being forced-fed material by the instructor.

Make sure your organization focuses more on learning than training. This important shift in emphasis will better serve your organization.

Chapter Wrap-Up

Chapter Wrap-Up

In this chapter you have learned:

- How to give a productive and successful seminar.

- How to provide effective on-the-job-training.

- Cross-training works because it allows employees to gain personal insight into co-workers responsibilities.

- A stand-in needs to be someone you feel is competent and that you would trust to operate your business when you are absent.

- How to know when training is the right solution.

- The difference between learning and training.

Chapter 5 – Pre-Planning Seminars

 PDF's of these forms are available online at:
www.osteryoungobrien.com
enter code: **OST+OBR=2010**

Successful Seminar Pre-Planning

What is the reason for the seminar? _____

_____

What do you hope to accomplish? _____

_____

What topics are you including in your seminar? _____

_____

_____

_____

_____

*How are you presenting (Power Point, Slides, Marker Board, Flip
Charts)?* _____

_____

*Have you included visuals in your presentation, such as props, music,
and/or images?* _____

Did you include logical steps for your audience to follow? _____

Did you use repetition where necessary? _____

*Have you tested your timing with the props and technology you plan
to use?* _____

*Did you allow time for audience interaction strategies such as
questions & answers sessions and role playing?* _____

Chapter 5 – Cross-Training & Stand-ins

Cross-Training

Do you feel like you have any "invaluable" employees? _____

Make a list of those employees and then decide who each person should cross-train with.

_____

_____

_____

_____

_____

Stand-ins

Who is your most reliable, competent, trustworthy, motivated employee? _____

Is this employee capable of being trained as a stand-in? _____
If they are, make a list of important roles they already understand and a list of roles they need more experience in.

_____

_____

_____

From this list, plan training times with the employee that work for both of you. _____

_____

_____

Ask yourself, "Will I actually let go and allow this person to fully act as my stand-in? _____
If yes, good. If no, why not? _____

_____

Chapter 5 – Take Aways & Action Steps

Take-Aways and Action Steps

1. _____

_____

Completion Date: _____

*Results:*_____

_____

2. _____

_____

Completion Date: _____

*Results:*_____

_____

3. _____

_____

Completion Date: _____

*Results:*_____

_____

4. _____

_____

Completion Date: _____

*Results:*_____

_____

5. _____

_____

Completion Date: _____

*Results:*_____

_____

Chapter 6

Identify, Nurture & Promote Key Players

● ●

Chapter At-A-Glance

By the end of this chapter you will know:

- Why to promote your employees.
- When to promote from within your current staff vs. finding a new employee.
- How to identify employees for promotion.
- The six traits of great employees.
- How to set up job progression in a small business.
- Why it is important to set a plan of transfer in a family business (Successful Succession Planning).

One of a business owner's main responsibilities is to identify talented employees and, through coaching, mentoring and education, prepare these employees for future promotion. It is impossible to over stress how important this concept is for every business.

With qualified labor in increasingly short supply, it is vital that business owners do all they can to keep their staff motivated and engaged. An excellent way to accomplish this is to encourage promotion within your organization.

Promoting from within gives you the opportunity

to identify potential leaders, nurture and advance them through your organization. In addition, promoting from within cultivates employee loyalty and can boost morale.

Another significant benefit is the savings associated with promoting from within versus hiring an outsider. In many cases, an otherwise qualified candidate may only be missing a simple skill set. In these cases, it is preferable to send the employee out for training or back to school rather than to bring a new employee in. Only when there is no one available internally to fill a position should you look outside of your business.

Take caution, however, one of the biggest mistakes you can make is to abruptly promote a member of a team to a management position over their former team members. This invariably creates a difficult situation. Staff has a hard time understanding that the promoted worker is no longer one of them. Also, it is usually difficult for the new manager to set aside friendship and

Business Owner's Responsibility

- Identify talented employees.

- Keep your staff motivated and engaged.

- Nurture and advance potential leaders in your staff.

- Equip your current staff with new skills by offering training/ education.

- Make sure other employees respect the authority of the newly promoted employee.

- Give your employee time to consider whether she will be comfortable with the new responsibilities that come with the promotion.

give out instructions. Making such a drastic leap in one day is a difficult adjustment for both the workers and the new manager. It can easily destroy the morale of the department.

Instead, promote in stages or steps, increasing responsibility over time. This allows both the new manager and the other workers time to become comfortable with the new arrangement.

The Planning Process

Every organization needs to have a plan in place for identifying promotable associates. Putting the plan in place before you need to fill a position helps prevent numerous difficulties after the fact.

The first step in this planning process is to identify those employees with leadership potential and skill. Just because someone is a hard worker does not necessarily mean that person can handle a higher level of responsibility. Look for people who get along with other staff members and who is more trusted and respected by others in the organization. This is not an exact science; however,

Loss of a critical employee

An entrepreneur with a large business was bemoaning his lack of candidates to take over critical positions after losing some key staff.

Jerry asked him, "Have you identified those people in your organization who are going to be the future leaders? Have you nurtured and coached these people so they will be ready to assume additional responsibility when it opens up?"

The entrepreneur said that he had not because he was too busy just trying to keep his business running. Besides, he said, he had thought the employees he was now trying to replace would be there forever. **Plan now. Identify key players now. Waiting can be costly.**

Identify Gaps & Fill Needs

Before you can identify key players for promotion you must first determine the needs or gaps your company has.

- A need or gap is the difference between where you want your company to be and its current situation.

    For example: If your current sales are $3,000,000 and your two-year goal is $4,500,000. You have a gap of $1.5 million dollars or, expressed another way, a need to fill in the gap between current sales and expected, required, or desired sales.

- Knowing what your gaps or needs are, allows you to identify the knowledge, skills, or attitudes (KSA's) you require to close or narrow the gaps.

- Once you know what your gaps are and you have identified the KSA's required to fill those gaps, then you can begin your quest to find employees to train, nurture, and promote, who either have those KSA's already or who have the capacity to acquire them.

- If no existing employees have the requisite skills, talents or capacities then consider hiring from the outside.

if, perchance, you select the wrong person, you will have learned much in the process.

After you have identified staff members for grooming, develop a plan to give them the coaching, mentoring, or education they require to develop the necessary skills for the future.

Some business owners fear creating a plan to identify key employees because they don't want to show favoritism to one associate over the others. You must, however, prepare the business for moving into the future. This idea should be communicated clearly and often to all staff. It is your obligation as a leader to ensure the future of the company is secure and that transitions occur smoothly, with minimal disturbance to the business.

As the leader of the organization you have an obligation to develop a cadre of trained staff ready to move into positions of authority. Identifying them early will make it much easier for them to assume their new roles because everyone will be expecting them to do so.

As you begin to identify your future leaders, you might learn that some staff, despite your assessment, are not capable of performing the new roles. When you realize this, you should, as compassionately as possible, let these employees know that they are not ready for promotion yet. Tell them that in the future, you might consider them again.

Uncomfortable Employee

Be sensitive to your employees. Don't suffer from "the fallacy of self projection." Just because you like a task or duty does not mean everyone will. Try to allow people to work and grow inside their skill sets.

An entrepreneur had an office manager (in title only) who really was a graphic artist. Because he was swamped, the owner of the business asked (really told) the graphic artist to become responsible for the collection of accounts receivable.

While the employee attempted to obey his boss, collecting past due accounts was not in his comfort area and the resulting stress began affecting his attitude at work.

The office manager was fully functional in his previously assigned role, but this change of roles took him way out of his comfort zone. Clearly, the office manager was a creative, people-person, but he could not function in a role that brought the stress associated with the abuse and rejection he received while contacting clients about their past due accounts.

Chapter 6 – 6 Traits of Great Employees

6 Traits of Great Employees

1 Honesty and Integrity:
Honest people are dependable people; you know how they will act in a situation, increasing trust, the basis of good business relationships. Employees with integrity set the standard for other workers to follow.

2 Consistency of Effort:
Great employees develop the ability to rise to the level of effort required to accomplish their current goal. Their consistency develops a positive cause-and-effect relationship between actions and results. An employee who has developed strong, positive habits will achieve strong, positive results.

3 Energy and a 'Can Do' Attitude:
Great employees have positive attitudes, fueling a nearly endless energy supply to accomplish goals. An employee's attitude sets the tone for everyone following him or her, so considering it is vital in the promotion process.

4 Confidence:
Strong faith in oneself (her beliefs and abilities) allows a great employee to act with confidence.

5 People Skills:
Great employees must enjoy being around people. Extreme introverts just do not do well in a business. Some qualities to look for are:
- The ability to accept and empathize with all people, regardless of their background or beliefs.
- The ability to share their time, energy, and resources with others in ways that encourage and motivate, knowing there are no secrets to success.

6 Balance and Moderation:
Balance allows strong employees to analyze situations and events with their full capacities. Moderation smooths out the extremes of emotions. Coupled with consistency, balance and moderation give individuals appropriate power over themselves, over those around them, and over situations.

Chapter 6 – Job Progression

When prospecting to fill positions in your organization, look first for ways you can promote from within, even if it means sending current employees out for more training. Don't allow one weak or nonexistent skill to keep you from promoting an otherwise qualified or potential manager.

When considering an employee for promotion, make sure to discuss the new task or position with the employee before simply making a unilateral decision. While business owners certainly have the right, within measurable legal limits, to tell an employee what to do, this strategy isn't always the best for employee morale or your grief quotient.

Candidates need sufficient time to process the idea of a major change. Associates up for promotion may feel quite uncomfortable

> **Power Quote!**
>
> *"It is one of the most beautiful compensations of this life that no one can sincerely try to help another without helping himself."*
> - **Ralph Waldo Emerson**

with the idea of greater responsibility. You must discern whether this employee needs encouragement from you, or whether they will truly be a square peg in a round hole. If the latter is the case, everyone will be miserable. It is important to understand when to push and when to hold back.

If you approach promotions and expansion determinedly and sensitively, you will find you have a happier and more productive staff as, ultimately, you will have the right people in the right jobs.

Job Progression

Frequently there is very little opportunity for upward mobility for employees of small businesses. That is, for many employees, as well as managers, of entrepreneurial businesses, there is just no room for promotion.

95

Chapter 6 – Job Progression

The owners of many small businesses just ignore this problem and hope their staff can live with being in the same positions for long periods of time. However, most employees just do not function well doing the same jobs with the same challenges year after year.

It is vital to consider developing ways which allow your employees to advance within your organization. This holds true even if you do not currently have higher positions available for them.

One effective way to open opportunities for advancement is to create a series of graduated steps within each job description. These steps should be based upon meaningful ways to evaluate success.

These incremental job advancement levels can be applied to any type of job where upper advancement is very limited (for instance, programmers). This type of job progression should be available to all administrative staff, too.

By developing steps with associated criteria for advancement, including longevity and testing, you give employees the ability to progress and the knowledge of what they have to do to get promoted within their job classification.

Of course, advancement will require you to reward each and every employee, but this need not be expensive. Many business owners and managers who follow this plan give employees an increase of just $500 a year for each step in the progression; however, they also give plenty of recognition when associates reach a new level of achievement, especially in front of their peers.

Recognition may include items like patches for

> **Power Tip!**
>
> *Consider cross-training to both instill variety in your employee's work routine and insure that the loss of one central person doesn't shut down your business.*

> **Progression Level Example**
>
> If you were in the heating and air conditioning business (or another, similar trade), you might create levels for your service technicians.
>
> Level One = Service Technician
> Level Two = Expert Technician
> Level Three = Master Technician
> Level Four = Certified Technician
>
> Knowing that it takes 7 years and four tests to progress from Service Technician to Certified Technician, for example, encourages employees to work for advancement, even though a company might not actually have any higher positions for them at the present.

uniforms and commendations during staff meetings. Another effective form of recognition is to post advancement news on a bulletin board for the entire staff to see. The company break room is a good place for this. You can also submit noteworthy achievements to your local paper or industry-wide magazines.

Finding ways to keep your employees advancing in their jobs, along with providing the requisite job skills, is a powerful and effective way to keep your workforce motivated and engaged.

Succession Planning

Family businesses are critical to our economy. Somewhere between 80 and 95% of all corporations are family owned. This accounts for more than 17 million businesses in the United States. In fact, 30% of all Fortune 500 companies and 60% of all public companies are family run. Additionally, 49% of the Gross Domestic Product comes from family firms.

Chapter 6 – Succession Planning

Successful Succession Planning

Without exception, the number one problem with family businesses is succession planning.

Transferring ownership from one generation to another is just plain difficult. It is a process which cannot be hurried.

However, if family businesses are going to survive into the future, then they must commit to developing a viable plan and sticking with it.

It takes courage to have a succession plan, but not having one has been the death knell of many a family business.

Clearly family businesses represent so much of what is right with our country and our economy. However, the number of family firms that last more than one generation is very low. Less than 30% of family businesses are transferred to the second generation and less than 15% reach the third generation.

Why is this? Entrepreneurs and business owners tend to, "keep a finger in the pie." They like to stay active and challenged. These individuals derive joy, satisfaction, and even their personal identity from their business.

While these qualities are what inspired these first-generation owners to create a successful family business in the first place, in the long term they can work against the firm when it is time for the next generation to step into management. Many family businesses talk about transfer of ownership to the next generation, but a plan is rarely laid out.

In transferring the responsibility to the younger family members, it is rarely a problem of the younger generation's reluctance to take over, or one of incompetence. Instead, it is the difficulty the older generation has in giving up control. Too often, young family members who feel ready to take the reins end up sitting in place for ten to fifteen years until the parent either becomes incapacitated or passes away. During this period, business generally declines because there is no new energy. And often the best person to ensure the future of the company leaves because she is tired of waiting.

If you are an entrepreneur who has started and built up your company, you must decide which is more important to you: staying in charge indefinitely, or the long-term success of the company you built from the ground up. Plan now. Create a timeline for a gradual transfer of power and implement that plan on time.

Letting Go

Letting go of the reins is difficult. To help you implement your succession plan, ask yourself and honestly answer this question.

"What is more important to me, the long term success and survival of this business, or my reluctance to let go?"

The survival of the business should be the priority.

Chapter Wrap-Up

Chapter Wrap-Up

In this chapter you have learned:

- Promoting employees keeps your staff motivated and engaged.
- The deciding factors when determining to promote from within vs. hiring someone new are:
  - Identify employees who already have needed qualifications.
  - Determine if an employee can be trained to fill a new position.
  - Determine if the employee can handle the extra responsibility of the new position.
  - If no one in your current staff fits, then someone new must be brought in.
- Great employees have the following traits: Honesty & Integrity, Consistency of Effort, Energy and a "Can Do" Attitude, Confidence, Good People Skills, and Balance & Moderation
- Have set levels with guidelines for progressing through the levels for employee promotion in small business where regular promotions are not available.
- Set up a succession plan and stick to it, in regards to retirement and transition in family owned, or small businesses. This allows time for everything to transfer over as effortlessly as possible without hurting the business itself.

Chapter 6 – Promoting Key Players

 PDF's of these forms are available online at:
www.osteryoungobrien.com

▬ Promoting Key Players ▬

What skills are required for the promotion position? _____
_____
_____

*What gaps are there to fill in your business? (Be exact and detail the
criteria you use to measure the required skills.)* _____
_____
_____

Is anyone on your staff already qualified? _____
*If yes, who and why? (Again, be specific. This is a performance situa-
tion, NOT a popularity contest!)* _____
_____

*Is anyone on your staff missing only a few specific skills that can be
learned to fill the position?* _____
Is yes, who? _____

What skills do they lack? _____
_____

What training/education can be done? _____
_____

Where can we get that training/education? _____

How much will the training/education cost? _____

How long will the training/education take? _____

Chapter 6 – Promoting Key Players

How will you measure the effectiveness of the training/learning process? _____
_____

When does the next training cycle or semester begin? _____
_____

If you choose an employee from within, will he be comfortable in the new position? _____
Have you spoken with him about it? _____
If no, what would possibly make him uncomfortable? _____
_____
Did you ask him? _____

What can be done to put the employee at ease to make it work for him?

_____
_____

*Will other employees work efficiently under the newly promoted individual?*_____
If not, who would you have the problem with? _____

What would the problem be?

_____
_____

How can you resolve the problem to make it work? Be proactive. Attempt to preemptively solve problems involved with internal promotions.

_____
_____

Chapter 6 – Promoting Key Players

Will you need to bring in a new employee? _____
If yes, what is your plan of action?

_____

_____

What will the job description be?

_____

What skill sets are a "must have" and which are "nice to have"?
"Must Have": _____

_____

"Nice to Have": _____

_____

What will the pay scale and benefits package be?

_____

_____

What will you answer if a prospect asks about promotion, both how fast and how far?

_____

_____

When do you want them to start? _____

> **Power Tip!**
>
> Create a customized "Promotion Page" for your company or each division. Use the one above as a guideline. Hold a workshop with those involved in the hiring process to explain the purpose and function of the form. A form like this can be VERY powerful - IF YOU USE IT!

Chapter 6 – Take-Aways & Action Steps

Take-Aways and Action Steps

1. _____

_____

Completion Date: _____

*Results:*_____

_____

2. _____

_____

Completion Date: _____

*Results:*_____

_____

3. _____

_____

Completion Date: _____

*Results:*_____

_____

4. _____

_____

Completion Date: _____

*Results:*_____

_____

5. _____

_____

Completion Date: _____

*Results:*_____

_____

Chapter 7

Generational Management

• •

Chapter At-A-Glance

By the end of this chapter you will know:

- How to work with the special needs and concerns of the Baby Boomer Generation.

- How to work with the special needs and concerns of Generation X.

- How to work with the special needs and concerns of Generation Y, a.k.a. Millennials.

- How to use the best of the different skill sets of a multigenerational work force to set up teams.

- How to work in a multigenerational work environment.

Tsunami alert! A tidal wave of generational change is on us and will last for more than a decade. How well you recognize and respond to these intergenerational issues will likely determine both your survival and level of success.

One of the biggest problems for business owners is finding employees. Today, depending on the products and services that your business provides, you could face an entirely new set of problems never encountered by earlier business owners.

As we rapidly move deeper into the 21st century we find four generations in the

Chapter 7 – Generational Dates

workforce: children of WWII veterans born before the war, the Baby Boomers born after that war, Generation X and the Millennials, also known as Generation Y. The prewar generation is rapidly retiring and the millennials are just as rapidly entering the workforce.

Why is now different? Why should you pay attention to generational differences? How could they possibly impact your business? These are all valid questions which we will work hard to answer in this chapter. Some of this material will challenge you. You might even deny that some of it is either real or important.

F.Y.I.

Below is information you should know before continuing with this chapter:

The generation of early children of the World War II veterans, born before the war, are not covered in this chapter due to the rapid rate at which they are retiring.

Generation Y will be referred to as the Millennials in this chapter so there is no confusion between Gen-X and Gen-Y.

Beware, and keep an open mind.

Generational Dates

These are general dates and there definitely is overlap in each direction.

Boomers	• Born between 1946 and 1964 • The Beatles & The Rolling Stones
Generation X	• Born between 1965 - 1982 • Duran Duran & Rap
Millennials & Gen-Y	• Born between 1983 - 2000 • Boybands & American Idol

Baby Boomers

Harry S. Dent is a Tampa, Florida based demographer *(www.hsdent. com)*. His specialty is Baby Boomers, whom he has studied at length and in depth. Based on his research, he has made many predictions about the economy. If his predictions are correct, we all better have a contingency plan.

Dent's basic premise is that, in 2010, the Baby Boom generation will begin to retire, opting for reduced social security benefits at 63 rather than waiting for full benefits. The retiring Boomers will begin a shift from productivity and savings to living off their savings and social security. If this scenario plays out as predicted, we will experience an incredible shrinkage of available human capital. If Harry Dent is right, then in the upcoming years there will be more jobs than people to fill them, especially in science, computers, and engineering.

Other economists believe Boomers will opt for "semi-retirement," working out of necessity long after they want to. Members of this generation who did not plan well or save enough for full retirement, will find themselves laboring part-time and/or at jobs with lesser pay or status. This longer working life will help avert some of the worker shortages that many economists forecast. It will also set up intergenerational conflicts if Boomers don't retire, as the following generations will not advance as fast as they would like.

Another issue in these forecasts is whether or not the Boomers will be able, physically and mentally, to continue to work even though they want or need to. This will cause potential discrimination issues for employers who notice a worker's reduced abilities.

Boomers' Focus

More than any other generation working today, Boomers often attach their identity to their work; what they do is who they are. Long hours to gain status, power, and "toys" are worth the effort.

The Boomers have difficulty relating to the Gen-X & Millennials' attitude that work is either an inconvenience or a necessary evil. To Boomers, work is life in many ways. To succeeding generations there is work and there is life and the two shouldn't overlap. They certainly don't want work interfering with their life.

Gen-X and the Millennials view work as a means to earn money to live the life they desire. Boomers never made this distinction.

Getting the generations to discuss attitudes and motivations might help them understand each other better. However, don't expect understanding to necessarily translate into lower conflict levels. Toleration (putting up with) is the first goal. When you achieve acceptance (okay with) you've done a superior job.

Working with Boomers

In recent years, CVS and Publix have all gone out of their way to increase the number of older workers in their labor pool. They realize that older workers want to continue to work as they age and have many positive attributes. For one, they do not call in with children problems. Numerous executives have attested that older workers surpassed their expectations.

Check www.Seniors4Hire.com for a listing of over 50,000 seniors. Certainly, not every older worker is going to be right for your business. However, making the effort to hire older workers is definitely worth a try; you may be surprised by how great a job they do.

▬ Boomers' Special Needs ▬

All communications fall into one of two categories: formal and informal. Neither form is right or wrong, just different. As such, they should be employed for different purposes. For entrepreneurs, this means communicating with each staff member in the way they are most comfortable.

Baby Boomers prefer both written and spoken language to be very formal. Use passive voice, few pronouns, and non-emotional verbs. For example, the following statement is structured in the formal mode appropriate for a Boomer:

"Details of the proposal are in the third cabinet."

However, if you wanted to convey the same information to a Gen-Xer or a Millennial, you would say something more like,

"I believe the speech details are in the third cabinet."

Accommodations

To help you retain Boomers and their deep institutional knowledge consider making some accommodations for them. As they age and their energy levels and mental stamina fade, these suggestions will help them remain productive:

1. Shorter work hours - start later and end earlier.

2. More vacation time - not necessarily with pay.

3. Bigger fonts on communications, higher audio volume, & brighter lights in rooms.

It is sometimes difficult for a manager to believe that you can't speak to everyone the same way. Look at generational communication differences in the same way you would

109

look at cultural differences. Each generation has its own language. Words and phrases that are completely innocuous to one generation might have quite a different meaning to another. For instance, what does "hook up" mean to you? To a Boomer it means "meet" or "get together," while to a Gen-Xer, it has a casual sexual connotation.

■ Approaches to Technology ■

Many people older than forty have a fear of computers, PDA's and other devices they consider to be "high tech." The problem with this fear is, these devices are no longer considered high tech. They are simply vital tools of the 21st century. Understanding how to use these tools is increasingly necessary, especially in the business sphere.

With these machines we can communicate instantaneously from anywhere in the world. The future holds an ever-increasing array of smaller, faster and more powerful machines and software.

Children and young adults generally have no fear of technology, having grown up with it. To them, software is just a plastic circle that contains the games they want to play.

Calculators are fast ways to get their homework done. Fax machines, e-mail and texting, save them the cost of a stamp (if they ever used one) when they have to write thank you notes to grandparents. For this demographic, computers are tools that allow interaction with the world of their choice, whether real or virtual, of their choice. They stay in touch and let the world know about their lives through avenues such as web 2.0, YouTube, and social networking sites like Facebook, MySpace, and Twitter.

The remaining few, prewar generation workers, who have experienced such dramatic change, view technology with trepidation. Many of them don't like technology believing it has contributed to the depersonalization of the world.

Because of their competitive nature, Boomers want to master technology. It is them against the machines.

Generation X are the gamers and want to enjoy technology.

Millennials, because technology has always been a part of their world, work to find ways to employ it as a tool, preferring texting to talking.

We are now in the information and knowledge age. To participate fully, your employees must be technologically literate. It is a good idea to map the age of your employees in general terms. This will help you develop a targeted approach for ongoing technological training.

Continuous training and upgrading of technology skills is not a luxury, it is a necessity. The speed and complexity of change is increasing and we must find ways to deal with it or risk falling behind or even becoming obsolete. Software upgrades, totally new programs, changed reporting

Boomer Basics

- Boomers like to talk about themselves and their interests.

- Many Boomers are now looking for deeper meaning in their lives.

- Living in the moment is very important and possibly the reason why they have planned so poorly for the future.

requirements, and many other events require that you, your company, and your employees stay current. This doesn't mean you should switch from what you currently have to the most recent new gizmo. It does mean that skills become outdated and successful firms should work to keep up.

Design your in-house learning and training to match the generational makeup of your workforce. One size, one approach will not fit all, unless you only employ a single generation. Customize your program if you can. The more flexibility and options you can offer, the better your chances of having an option that will fit your people. If you are a small company with only a few employees, allow them to have input into training where practical. All employees, from any generation, like to have a say in what impacts them.

Generation X

Generation X: We hear this group called by many names. Most of these names imply a group of confused, disjointed, uneducated misanthropes. Perhaps the people who coined the term "Lost Generation" hadn't taken the time to learn this generation's language.

While some of them are "misfits." Every generation has its share, and we need them. Often, the ones who don't fit the mold make the most significant contributions. We have all heard the admonition to "think outside the box." Misfits don't have a box.

The truly defining attribute of Gen-X, though, is maturity beyond their years. These people had to grow up fast, many of them as latch-key kids, who were home

Gen-X Basics

- Unlike Boomers or Millennials, Gen-X really has no heroes.

- Gen-X meets and dates in groups to start with. "Dating," usually implies the relationship has taken on a sexual aspect. So be careful before you ask if anyone is dating someone.

- They will likely have 12 or more careers during their working life.

alone after school. Some of these young men and women were the primary caregiver to younger brothers and sisters in a single-parent home.

This group tends to be impetuous. They want answers and solutions now. Waiting for a bogged-down bureaucracy to make decisions is very frustrating for Gen-Xers. They have dedication, energy, and a practical, to-the-point approach to thinking.

Yes, in many ways they are "in your face." Gen-Xers see no value in circuitous talk. They want interaction, not dictum. They want to be a part of an interactive group that learns and grows by doing. While this age group believes they can comprehend and accomplish several activities at once (i.e., multi-tasking), credible research suggests this is both a myth and counterproductive.

These people use computers and PDA's like another appendage, and have no fear of technology. They relish it as an opening to new worlds, making life easier, more fun, and more complex.

Gen-Xers' Focus

Generation X believes they are able to multi-task. They contend they can do more than one activity at a time: e-mail, listen to music, type a paper, etc.

There is one major problem with multi-tasking:

Mono-tasking

"Mono-tasking is the lost art of doing one thing well, while being fully present, and fully focused, without guilt, loss, frustration, boredom, or anger. In a culture and world where it is commonplace and even "cool" to be constantly multi-tasking and trying to do everything at once, there is good reason to slow down and focus."

-Dr. J.M. Halderman

http://www.hyperstress.com/donotmultitask

except for the simplest and most menial activities it doesn't work.

There is very solid psychological research that shows that attempts at multi-tasking can cost up to forty percent in productivity vs. mono-tasking (doing one action to completion before starting a new project).

The problem stems from the time it takes our minds to adjust to the new rules of the second or third activity.

The more complex the task the greater the cost in terms of productivity.

▬ Gen-Xers' Special Needs ▬

As mentioned earlier, you must recognize the impact of generational differences on communication style. For instance, where Baby Boomers need formal communications, members of Gen-X respond better to the exact opposite. An informal style that uses active voice, pronouns, and plenty of emotional verbs is best for these age groups. Remember, they were taught to have "high self-esteem," just because they are who they are. This is very different than the self-esteem based on merit and accomplishment that Boomers value.

The sentence,

"The analysis was done by three of our staff,"

is an example of the formal mode. If you were communicating with a Baby Boomer, this is how you would structure the statement. However, if you wanted to say the same thing to a Gen-Xer, you would say something more like,

"I am pleased to say that three of our staff wrote this excellent report."

The second sentence is much more upbeat and conveys the feeling necessary to that will bolster their sense of self-esteem.

To keep Gen-Xers (those born between 1965 and 1982) engaged, you cannot tell them step-by-step how to do the job. Once they have an understanding of the work environment, Gen-Xers function best when given only an objective and limited guidance. This approach is an offshoot of the educational experiment called constructivism. This approach emphasized process over accuracy, speed or economic considerations. When you allow individuals or teams to work with limited "how-to," instructions and little direct guidance, be sure to have a frequent feedback system in place. This will allow you to monitor progress for direction, adherence to objectives, time taken and costs incurred.

Gen-Xers' Concerns

A generational concern for Gen-X, which is just now becoming evident, is they might be passed by for promotions. As a generation, they might never "hold the reins of power."

If Boomers stay on the job an extra five to ten years, when they finally do retire, many Millennials will be ready to take over the Boomers' positions of power. Millennials, who will be at least as well trained as Generation X, will jump over them. Additionally, Millennials will be at a lower or equivalent pay scale, making them attractive candidates to employers.

This will cause a new set of problems and issues for managers and business owners.

▰ Millennials/Generation Y ▰

If you are not already managing a Generation Y/ Millennial Generation staff, you will eventually. These are young people just entering the workforce who were born between 1982 - 2000. They will, in time, become the backbone of our labor force. The Millennial's behavior and motivation are very different from either Generation X or the Baby Boomers. You must understand what motivates them and their behaviors, and what they want from the work environment if you are to have a successful professional relationship with the Millennial generation.

Obviously, this group is much more tech-savvy. They grew up with a continual rapid growth in technology. Notice how many of them get their news off the web rather than from printed media. In many ways, these employees and future employees consider technology as their birthright and a tool.

One thing that makes

> ### Power Quote
>
> *"I suggest each of you make friends with some of the youngest generation. Be open-minded and ready to learn. They are very good teachers."*
> **-Tim O'Brien**

managing the Millennials unique is that they desire meaningful work. They want a job that will not only provide financial gain and professional opportunities, but one they know will have a positive impact on the greater community. Millennials are looking for significant purpose in their work experience that transcends monetary reward.

They are also unafraid of moving from job to job. Researchers expect the average Millennial to have twenty or more different careers. Clearly, job security is not their goal. By far, one of the most important things to remember in dealing with Millennials is that they are not necessarily loyal to the company they work for. They are also aggressive in their financial and company goals.

With the demand for workers increasing over the next two decades, you must understand what motivates Millennials so you can take the necessary steps to both recruit and retain them. **Remember what makes a Millennial tick: meaningful work, rapid advancement possibilities, and the opportunity to be heard.**

Millennials' Focus

Millennial Basics

- Millennials grew up in day care. They like teams and consensus.
- Millennials are less violent than previous generations.
- Millennials understand life-long learning but are in no hurry to get out of school or get married.
- Millennials are very family oriented.

In order to understand Millennials, you must realize that they are the children of Baby Boomers, who really value education, so Millennials clearly understand the importance of advanced learning. This generation will want jobs that allow them to grow educationally.

Millennials strive for the flexibility they did not have growing up. Typically, parents of this generation wanted them to be involved in many different activities. As children, they were taken to dance and music classes, participated in sports, and then did homework at night. Desiring to escape from this over-scheduling has made Millennials aim for freedom from fixed constraints. The work environment must change to accommodate these types of demands by offering options such as telecommuting and very flexible working hours.

117

Millennials' Special Needs

The lack of loyalty and longevity in today's workforce is a bigger problem than you might think. From a monetary perspective, it is important to hold on to your skilled workers as the cost to retrain and replace them is so high. Also, intuitional knowledge lost when long-time employees die, retire or leave can devastate a company. So, how does an employer increase loyalty in an environment that does not encourage this value.

One action that does appear to make a difference is the development of family-friendly workplaces which recognize the importance of the family in their employees' lives.

There are a number of ways you can develop a family-friendly workplace. One of the most common of these is offering flex-time hours. Flex-time means that the specific hours worked are flexible as long as the total weekly requirement is met. There are two basic types of flex hours. The first is to allow flexibility in starting and quitting times which, once set, remain fixed. Then, there is flexibility of hours from day to day and week to week. The first type obviously

Suggestions

- Millennials come into the workforce confident and feeling ready to lead. Tap this attitude and enthusiasm by asking for input at all practical junctures.
- Millennials want instant feedback - now - so be sure to comment and praise often.
- Millennials expect rapid promotions, remember when they were in competitions as youths everyone got a trophy. As suggested in Chapter 6, breakdown each major promotion into many small incremental promotions.

allows for better planning.

Another way to be family-friendly is to help employees with their childcare concerns. One solution, many large companies have opted for is installing on-site childcare centers. Often this benefit alone has attracted workers that could have easily gone elsewhere for employment. Another solution is to pay a portion of workers' childcare costs or work with nearby centers to provide a discount or other special considerations, such as flexible drop-off and pickup times, to your employees.

Millennials' Concerns

When employees look sloppy or are inappropriately dressed, it communicates that sloppy work or inappropriate behavior is tolerated. Dress codes are a company's best way of managing the appearance of its employees.

A number of issues, however thorny, should be addressed in your company's dress code. When establishing your policies, first think about what you consider to be appropriate dress. If an employee is working in a factory, jeans are clearly appropriate, but jeans in an office setting may not be. Type and condition of clothing should also be considered

> **"I'm outta here!"**
>
> - It is hard to overstate how willing Millennials are to change jobs or even just stop working for awhile to travel or volunteer.
> - Keep them engaged.
> - Keep them in teams. This provides a more cohesive unit for them than a company.

when establishing your dress code. Address revealing clothing, as well as shirts with messages that are not in good taste. Even in a business with a casual work environment, clothing should be pressed. Torn, dirty or frayed clothing is unacceptable. A significant trend with Millennials (those born after 1982), tattoos and body piercings have increased in prevalence. Both the number of people getting them and the amount and size of the tattoos and piercings themselves has grown. Somewhere between thirty-five to fifty percent of Millennials have tattoos or body piercings.

When creating your company's dress code, consider that one of the best ways to get employees to embrace a new rule is to seek their input up front. Ask both employees and customers what they consider to be appropriate dress. Once you have collected this data, develop a draft policy and circulate it among your staff for their thoughts. You will probably never get 100% buy-in, however, giving employees of all generations a voice in its development, will contribute to their willingness to embrace a dress code.

Multi-Generation Staff

"The Fallacy of Self-Projection" occurs when we take an experience, belief, or assumption that we accept as accurate, and generalize it, mistakenly assuming everyone feels as we do.

The fallacy of self-projection causes much of the misunderstanding between generations. Each group has its own general system of behavior and

Snowflakes

"Generations are like snowflakes. They look similar but each is unique. Accentuate commonality and de-emphasize differences."
- Tim O'Brien

moral code. Problems occur when one group feels another group would be fine if they just adopted the first group's thinking and way of life.

Chapter 7 – Self-Projection

Self-Projection

Some possible causes of the Fallacy of Self-Projection are

- One generation feeling superior to another.
- A lack of exposure to, or ignorance of, differing points of view due to voluntary or involuntary isolation within one's own group.
- A strict adherence to a system of beliefs that dictates and tolerates no deviation (for example, while an older worker might hold a strong belief in referring to a superior by their last name and title, younger workers often feel more comfortable relating to their boss on a first-name basis).
- A viewpoint that allows no consideration of other systems or lifestyles.

We like to feel we are right, and know how to behave correctly in our profession. We also like to believe we are tolerant and inclusive toward our co-workers. However, feeling and believing something doesn't make it accurate or true.

It is not reasonable to expect everyone to cooperate and to get along. The world's population is more than six billion people. That number nearly guarantees that we will encounter polar opposites in our workplace. We will find ourselves with people or groups that believe, follow, and support life styles, beliefs, and mores diametrically opposed to our own or the groups we associate with.

When your staff is comprised of multiple generations, assess what you have to work with. Try to identify the strengths, weaknesses, aptitudes, and attitudes of each person involved. Be very careful not to allow this exercise to devolve into stereotyping. The purpose is to realize the skill sets and beliefs of your staff. Then, develop a plan to work with your team to achieve the priorities and goals of your business.

Once you understand

Chapter 7 – Staff Shortages

the profile of your group, find common ground upon which to build a consensus. Work towards as much agreement as practical. Depending on the size of your staff and the number of projects available, create teams around common interests wherever possible.

A caveat here: keep balance, quality, and skill in mind. A team who can get along quite well and has much in common, is certainly good. However, if that team is incompetent, it may hinder your company's goals. Strive for affinity, but require competence too.

■ Dealing with Staff Shortage ■

From approximately 2005 the number one worry of business owners we speak with is how to fill their staffing needs. Since 2007, when we moved into a tenacious recession, some of these concerns have temporarily abated. However, their concern is warranted because the perfect storm for a labor shortage is scheduled

to hit as soon as hiring picks up, which is expected to be sometime in 2011. Many Baby Boomers will be leaving the labor force. Combined with smaller family sizes and a growing economy, it has been forecasted that the demand for workers will outstrip the supply.

Don't be an Ostrich II

All of this generational information is not just smoke & mirrors. There are differences between generations - one size does not fit all. Aging Boomers will get slower both mentally & physically - prepare for and make allowances for it. Millennials will likely overrun Gen-Xers. Be prepared.

Chapter 7 – Staff Shortages

> **How to deal with a staff shortage.**

How do you cope with this?

- ***Get as much technology in place as possible to replace the need for workers.*** I have seen well-managed firms increase their sales, maintain their customer service and reduce their labor force simply by employing new technology. This is a major point. You can increase productivity through appropriate use of technology. This is working smarter.

- ***Try to review the tasks each worker performs and determine which of these can be transferred to a computer.*** You will be surprised to discover how many tasks performed by a person can be shifted to computers.

- **For every task ask**: "How can we change this? How can we simplify this process?" And most importantly, "What would happen if we dropped this task?" It might stun you how often the answer to this question is "nothing important."

- ***Another action to consider is outsourcing some of your routine operations.*** A number of companies in this or other countries are able to provide these services. Many firms outsource their programming and customer-service duties to India a savings of fifty percent or more. Many firms allow a company to outsource payroll functions. However, due to cultural and language differences being too great, this is a trend that many companies have reversed, especially concerning the outsourcing of HR functions.

The more of these adaptations you can implement now, the better positioned you will be to avoid future work force shortages.

Chapter Wrap-Up

Chapter Wrap-Up

In this chapter you have learned:

- Boomers need spoken and written language to be very formal.

- Boomers find their identity in their work.

- Technology does not come naturally to Boomers.

- Generation X needs spoken and written language to be informal.

- Generation X believes they can multi-task.

- Generation X fears they may be passed up for promotions for the younger Millennials (Gen-Y).

- Millennials like a set fixed schedule of when they start and stop, but also like it to be flexible as long as all the required work is completed in time for deadlines.

- Millennials understand the importance of advanced learning.

- Millennials lack loyalty and longevity in the workplace. They will quickly move on for better pay and/or hours.

- If your staff is large enough, group employees together who work well as a team.

FYI! PDF's of these forms are available online at:
www.osteryoungobrien.com
enter code: **OST+OBR=2010**

Chapter 7 – Company Skill Sets

Use the chart below to collate and match people to jobs. Use this as a way to get input and access the skill sets the company possesses. For a larger or extra copy visit *www.osteryoungobrien.com*.

					Idea Generation	Fundraising	Community Contacts Liason	Skill Sets / Department
								Marketing and / or PR
								Banking, Finance or Accounting
								Organizational & Leadership

Chapter 7 – Employee Skill Sets

Use this second chart to allow employees to fill in their own self perceived skill sets. Then have managers fill out the form also, as a cross reference. For a larger or extra copy visit *www.osteryoungobrien.com*.

					Fred	Sue	Bob	Skills Sets / Employee
								Community Contacts Liasion
								Fundraising
								Idea Generation

"We are not animals. We are not a product of what has happened to us in our past. We have the power of choice."
- Stephen Covey

Chapter 8

Change Management

• •

Chapter At-A-Glance

By the end of this chapter you will know:
- The four steps to Change Management.

- Why it is important to keep your business current with your market.

- Why to keep an eye on the competition.

- What grapevine rumors are, how to watch for them, and how to stop them.

- Why and how to keep your employees informed.

- Why it is important to keep current on technology.

- Why continuing education for you and your employees is critical.

- How and why to stay current on federal laws regarding employees and your business.

- How to produce a Disaster Plan for your business and your employees.

Several years ago, some entrepreneurs started a company. For the first ten years, it flourished both in terms of sales and profits. However, over the next seven years, performance eroded, with sales falling by at least ten percent a year and profits declining even faster. Additionally, in the last two years, profits had turned negative, and the owners were forced to borrow funds from the bank just to keep the operation going. The owners realized that they could not turn the company around fast enough to stave off bankruptcy.

What happened to this company? For the first ten years of operation, they enjoyed a market with very little competition and very high margins. Around seven years ago, however, a significant number of new competitors

Four Steps to Change Management

1. **Write down your plan.** This is not just a mental exercise. Look at the plan, question it, and keep writing until you develop a sense of clarity.

2. **What you can describe, you can conquer.** Once you've taken note of the weaknesses in your plan, begin to think of solutions for them. What are options and alternate courses of action? Do you need to rethink your position? List the answers; develop a proactive approach to implementing them.

3. **Make mid-course corrections frequently.** Reinforce your good decisions. Reduce the impact of your bad ones. Think and act; don't succumb to the "paralysis of analysis."

4. **Get help when you can't figure out a situation by yourself.** Every field has its experts. Find them and use them appropriately. This is a sign of intelligence not weakness.

Chapter 8 - You Can't Avoid It

began entering the market. Their competitors offered better products and services, albeit at a higher price. The new companies were able to gain market share through effective advertising, and a top-notch sales team, neither of which could be afforded by the first firm.

When the owners of the company noticed both the presence of competitors in the market and their own declining sales, they refused to act, rationalizing they had been operating successfully in their way for the past ten years. They failed to realize the market was changing and they were not.

In fairness, the owners mistakenly thought that this change was going to be temporary, and that their competitors' higher prices would eliminate them from the marketplace. However, after seven years, the competitors just got bigger and bigger. Still this firm did not adapt.

In order to adapt, you must recognize any changes in your market. In this case, the owners either did not see what was happening or refused to see it. Except for the owners' mistaken assumptions, there was no reason this firm should have failed. Not only did they believe that the new competition could not be sustained, but they also believed that their way of doing business was the correct way. Their stubbornness prevented them from recognizing the changes and acting on what they saw. For them, denial was

> ### You can't avoid it.
>
> *"All is flux, nothing exists but change."*
> **- Heraclitus**
>
> *"There is nothing wrong with change if it is the right decision."*
> **- W. Churchill**
>
> *"Be the change you wish to see in the world."*
> **- M. Gandhi**
>
> *"Change is inevitable - except from vending machines."*
> **- R. C. Gallagher**

deadly.

The law of natural selection applies to business, too; the market punishes those firms that are not fit. You must be willing to recognize when conditions are changing, and, when they are, you must adapt. Those firms that can continually adapt are the ones that will survive. Being aware of change, allows you to devise a plan to adapt to it.

It's been said that only two things are certain: death and taxes. However, there is a third unavoidable event: change. Most businesses change repeatedly. These alterations may range from goals to compensation packages. To survive, your business must adapt and not just react. Be on the lookout for change. Expect it. Then, when it happens develop your adaptive plan for surviving and thriving.

Employee Issues

Change is so pervasive that you need to understand how help your associates accept change rather than fight it. Suppose your firm is considering a merger or acquisition. When and what should you tell your staff?

Suppose you are considering selling your business. When and what should you tell your staff? These are some of the critical decisions business owners must make on a fairly frequent basis. However, too often

business owners get so excited and distracted when they are involved in a deal they forget all about the many employee issues that arise during the process.

It is very important to apprise the employees as to what is happening. Having discussions behind closed doors or late at night tends to cause employees to think the worst, and often causes rumors. Most employees equate change with loss. This is neither good nor bad, but just

Chapter 8 - Grapevine Rumors

the human condition of assuming that change is bad. That is why it is important to keep them as informed as practical. While the sensitivity of the issues may prevent you from disclosing everything, divulge as much as prudence and non-disclosure agreements allow.

There is a point where you have to be courageous and tell your employees about your plans. For example, the latest point you can choose to disclose proposed mergers, acquisitions or sellouts to your employees is when you begin the legal paper work. When explaining an upcoming change to your staff, you do not need to go into voluminous detail. Rather, focus on the issues that impact them. Think through and keep in mind what is and is not relevant for staff to know.

Grapevine Rumors

There are four types of grapevine rumors:

- **Wish fulfillment** - identifying the wishes and hopes of employees.
- **"Bogey rumors"** - exaggerating employees' fears and concerns.
- **"Wedge-drivers"** - aggressive, unfriendly and damaging. They split groups and dissolve allegiances.
- **"Home-stretchers"** - anticipating final decisions or announcements. They tend to fill the gap during times of ambiguity.

- Author/Consultant,
Kim Harrison

Rumors serve no constructive purpose unless disinformation is your goal - have a company policy and procedure for dealing with and defusing rumors.

■ Selling Changes to Your Staff ■

When trying to get your associates to understand and accept an upcoming change, it is best to convey the idea to them on an emotional level. Make eye contact, use personal language, and a softer tone of voice. Change evokes emotions and attempting to convince people to accept change on a rational or logical basis is rarely effective.

Another way to encourage employees to accept change is to bring them into the decision process whenever feasible. After deciding to develop a financial incentive program, for instance, some business owners ask employees for their input. Frequently, employees do not reply to requests for input, but you still need to give them the opportunity to make suggestions. If they later complain or object, you can gently remind them that they did not offer input when given the opportunity to do so.

A third method of helping your employees buy-in to a proposed change is to create a committee or task force of employees to wrestle with the problems and propose solutions and details associated

> ### Upcoming Change
> - Convey the change on an emotional level.
> - Let employees have input in the decision, if possible and practical.
> - Create an employee based committee to help with the change.
> - If the rate of change is under your control don't make the change too fast.

> ### Try honesty
> If you have critical information to share with your employees, do it in the most direct, sensitive and honest way possible. They can handle the truth.

with the upcoming change. Don't use this approach unless you are willing to consider the committee's findings. Some companies use this approach thinking that they can either guide the committee to the desired decision or they believe (or hope) the committee will come up with the "only logical choice," on their own. Don't count on this outcome.

When making changes, you must make sure that you do not proceed too fast. If transitions are made too rapidly, employees may refuse to leave their comfort zone. If you have big changes to accomplish in a short time frame, sell those changes to your employees in steps or stages. Getting your employees to accept change seems to work much better when administered in small doses. Remember the way to eat an elephant is "one bite at a time."

Technology

Technology is changing rapidly! A little over twenty years ago, if you went to buy a computer, you might have stopped at a Radio Shack. The computer would have had a few kilobytes of RAM and a cassette tape to store information. It would not have had hard disks or even disk drives only "floppies." Computers have come a long way!

Technology has made our world much smaller and faster. We are only a portion of a second away from anywhere in the world via the Internet. PDA's, cell phones, computers, FAX machines, international beepers, voicemail, e-mail, call

Technology Safety

Never, ever, text while driving. If you think you can multi-task, you're mistaken.

Your momentary lapse of attention could be fatal to you or others.

Please think about others when you drive and text.

133

Chapter 8 - Hands-Free Devices

waiting, video conferencing and the various social media networks are all an integral part of modern life. Remember this simple rule concerning technology: use it to your advantage, but don't allow it to enslave you. Each device has an "off button." You choose whether or not to be available 24/7. Like most tools, technology can be either a blessing or a curse. How you use it makes the difference.

Some business owners and managers attempt to add new technology and fail miserably. In order to be useful technology must solve a real problem. It must improve your company, your life and the life of your employees. Too often, sales people will try to sell you technology on factors that are not real issues. For example, while speed of a computer is important, excess speed may not add value to your business. It is analogous to having a car designed for long hauls when you only drive in the city. Buy only what you can use

"Hands Free"

When "hands-free," devices first came out I got one right away. I thought I was pretty cool until I was cured by a big laugh at my own expense. While making a deposit at a bank's drive-through, I was talking away on my cell phone as I put my deposit into the tube."

The women behind the glass wall giggled and pointed. They were sure I was one brick short of a load. Feeling smug, I picked up my cell phone and smiled as I pointed to it, putting an end to their surmise. The laugh was on me. I had to bring them back their deposit tube since I wasn't paying attention and drove off with it.

Using "hands-free," technology does take a little getting used to, however the safety factor makes it worth it worth the effort.

- Tim O'Brien

while allowing for expansion or the ability to "plug in," new applications. However, don't spend too much now. Technology becomes outdated and falls in price quickly.

> **Blue Tooth**
>
> Today, many people walk around with their "blue tooth," hands-free earpiece as if it is surgically attached to their ear.
>
> Being "hands-free" is more popular now. Not everyone uses it, though some states now require it and there is national legislation pending.
>
> If you are going to talk on the phone while driving, use hands-free technology. It is the safe approach to talking while driving.

Keeping Up

State regulatory agencies require most professionals to complete a certain amount of continuing education. Lawyers have to complete thirty hours over three years to renew their license. Medical doctors, including specialists like brain surgeons, are required to complete forty hours over a two-year period. Certified public accountants must complete eighty hours over two years. Why is this? Regulatory agencies know that the critical skills needed in a profession fade away with time. Additionally, continuing education courses introduce professionals to new concepts and new technologies. Finally, by taking an individual out of his or her routine to participate in an educational experience, the regulatory agencies hope to increase the professional's motivation and enthusiasm for his or her own business.

Each business owner and manager should take time off for his or her own education. Holding the erroneous belief that you already know all there is to know about your products, services, customers, or associates may endanger your business. Many business

135

owners and managers send their employees to regular training, but neglect their own. You must take the time to learn new skills and technology.

There are many classes addressing necessary new skills, technologies and laws for business owners that are applicable to all businesses. Some of these are:

1. **Accounting software (e.g. QuickBooks)**
2. **Internet usage and web sites**
3. **Legal (e.g. employee and environment)**
4. **Managing employees**
5. **Technology trends**

Additionally, most trade associations offer courses. Some of the topics considered in these trade meetings are: selling techniques that really work, hot selling products/ services, and current, significant

> ### Life-Long Learning
>
> Develop and maintain a life-long learning program. This is a vital key to your continued personal growth, development and success.
>
> *"But I don't have time."*
>
> I hear so many people complain. *"Yes you do,"* is my standard answer.
>
> *"How?"*
>
> This is the next word out of their mouths. *"One hour at a time,"* is my next standard answer.
>
> One hour per day, five days per week, forty-eight weeks per year is 240 hours of focused effort on the subjects of your choice. That is six full, forty hour weeks.
>
> What could you accomplish with six weeks of concentrated effort? Plenty!
>
> - Tim O'Brien

trends in the industry.

Investing to increase your knowledge and skills will pay substantial dividends to you, to your associates, to your customers, and to your bottom line. Make it a personal goal to spend forty hours each year in classes, learning information you can utilize in your business.

Chapter 8 - Legal

We have a choice. We can choose to broaden the scope of ways we keep in touch with the world around us, or, we can risk becoming isolated, bypassed, and so specialized in our knowledge that we can only communicate with others in our field. Have you ever been to a party and been the only one who is not an attorney or physician?

There has never been so much information available. Take advantage of it through books, magazines, newspapers, blogs, search engines and other resources on the Internet. The more you accurately learn, the more information and resources you have available to make informed decisions. This will also keep you out in front of nearly everyone else you know. Too many people become complacent and, at some point, feel they've "got it made." At that moment they begin to fall behind. Remember the law of entropy: *"That which does not grow begins to die."*

Legal

According to federal law, even if you have just one employee, you must abide by eleven to fifteen laws, including:

- Fair Labor Standards Act (FLSA) - regulates the wage and hour laws for employers in the public and private sectors.
- Immigration Reform & Control Act (IRCA) – requires all newly hired employees to complete I-9 forms, in which they attest that they are legally allowed to work in the U.S.
- Equal Pay Act - requires employers to pay all employees equally for equal work, regardless of their gender.
- Uniformed Services Employment & Reemployment Rights Act

of 1994 - requires employers to reinstate employees upon their completion of military service and prohibits employers from discriminating against individuals because of past, present, or future membership in a uniformed service.

Once you hit the fifteen employee limit then you need to worry about the:

- Americans with Disabilities Act (ADA) - prohibits discrimination against qualified individuals with disabilities in employment, public accommodations, transportation, state and local government services and telecommunications.
- Title VII of the Civil Rights Act of 1964 - makes it unlawful for an employer to discriminate against any individual with respect to his or her compensation, terms, conditions, or privileges of employment on the basis of race, color, religion, sex or national origin.

"I didn't know that!"

Some people say, "it is better to ask forgiveness than permission."

- If you ascribe to this attitude be very careful when applying it to labor laws, rules and regulations.
- You expose yourself to severe, punitive fines and even jail time if you carelessly expose your clients or employees to danger or health hazards.
- Don't risk a problem, stay current and aware of the proper practices and procedures for dealing with employees.

With twenty or more employees, you have to be concerned with:

- Age Discrimination in Employment Act (ADEA) - promotes the employment of older persons based on ability rather than age, and prohibits arbitrary age discrimination. It protects persons age forty and older and applies to both private and public employers.

With fifty or more employees, you have to be concerned with:

- Family and Medical Leave Act - Employees must be allowed (up to) twelve unpaid workweeks during a one year time period for caring for an immediate family member, birth and care of a new born, adoption, or serious health issues.

And that's just in dealing with employees! Obviously, there are myriads of laws that you need to be aware of in business, as the cost for noncompliance can be huge.

"We are here to help you"

A very detailed and informative website by the Federal Government on employee rules and regulation is :
www.business.gov/business-law/employment

This is one site where the government really is "there to help you." Take advantage of it.

Disaster

What if there were a fire at your home or office, and you experienced total loss? How would it affect you? How would you respond? What would you do?

Sometimes, unforeseen or uncontrollable events thwart the best laid plans. Having a worst-case scenario plan is vital. You need to consider what actions would you take

O.S.H.A

Another type of disaster is a company-specific event such as the death of an employee, toxic spill or other safety or health related catastrophe.

Be familiar with the portions of O.S.H.A. that relate to your company.

if everything went wrong, or if nothing happened as it should, or if disaster struck.

It is paramount for business owners and managers to devise disaster plans for their companies. Part of your plan should address not only what happens if your area is hit by a disaster, such as hurricane, earthquake, tornado, or terror strike, but also what might occur if some other area that has a profound impact on your business gets hit? After Hurricane Katrina, many firms could not buy the products they needed because the products were manufactured near New Orleans. The time to plan is now, rather than waiting for a storm or other disaster to be upon you.

▬ Making a Disaster Plan ▬

One of the first considerations in a disaster plan is your staff. If your employees evacuate for safety reasons, you need a way to keep track of them. Cell phones may not

Make a list, check it twice

Another very valuable government sponsored website is:
FEMA (Federal Emergency Management Agency)
www.fema.gov/plan/index.shtm
It has guides and guidelines for disaster preparedness for anything you can think of:

* Dam Failure	* Nuclear Explosion
* Earthquake	* Terrorism
* Fire or Wildfire	* Thunderstorm
* Flood	* Tornado
* Hazardous Material	* Tsunami
* Heat	* Volcano
* Hurricane	* Wildfire
* Landslide	* Winter Storm

Chapter 8 - Pre-Planning

Pre-Planning

1. Plan to ensure, no matter what the disaster, there will be no loss of life. Physical property can be replaced. People cannot.

2. Check your insurance coverage annually. Discuss the coverage with your insurance agent to be sure you keep up with current costs. Pay special attention to your contents coverage.

3. Video your home, or homes, and office. Pictures of each room of the building will greatly help with an insurance claim. However, pictures cannot take the place of a slow, total video view of the structure. As you film each room or area, speak in a clear voice. Describe every item you see down to the smallest part. If you remember where you purchased the item, mention that. If you know how much the item cost, detail that. There is no item too small. There is no detail too insignificant. If you have to list page after page of items for reimbursement from the insurance company, you will understand the wisdom of this suggestion. Store your video and pictures away from the home or office, in your safety deposit box at your bank or in another secure location.

4. Consider whether to rebuild or move elsewhere in the event of total loss.

Chapter 8 - When Disaster Does Strike

"The best laid plans of mice and men, often go astray."

- Robert Burns

Regardless of our best intentions, hopes and plans, disasters sometimes do happen.

If your company is impacted by an external disaster your "disaster action plan," should cover at least the basics for protecting people and property and getting the business functioning afterward.

If your company causes a disaster, contact your attorney, your insurance agency and be proactive in dealing with it.

be your best bet. After a natural disaster, cell phone towers in the devastated areas may be over-loaded or damaged and unable to reroute calls. Depending on the size of your business, you may want to consider purchasing satellite phones for top executives. Satellite phones are unaffected by local conditions, so staff can call in to get messages and status updates. Some firms have toll-free numbers so employees can call in for information. Keeping track of employees whereabouts and contact information is very important.

In case of a hurricane, remember your staff will need adequate time to board up, or otherwise protect, their property and evacuate. Those incredible traffic jams shown on the news as folks tried to get out of Houston before Hurricane Rita hit should remind you of how critical it is to get your staff out of the danger area as soon as possible. There is usually no reason to delay unless you are in the hurricane supply business or work with medical or emergency support teams.

Make sure your company's physical structure is as safe as possible. You can put up pre-made plywood

Chapter 8 - Disaster Planning

storm shutters quickly and inexpensively. Also, you should plan to protect valuable equipment inside your building.

One of the most critical actions is to have a plan for saving your records and important papers. A computer backup is not sufficient. You must make sure your backup is out of harm's way before disaster strikes. You must also know how it works. Periodically check your system to ensure it is working and that you are completely familiar with it. Also, clearly define what paperwork must be copied and where these records are to be stored. Some of the original information which should be kept in a safe place are insurance policies, employee and customer data bases, mortgages, title information, and personnel files. Make a detailed list of your critical information, how you have safeguarded it and where you've stored it. "I meant to do that," won't help later.

There are firms that specialize in remote data storage. While many people do not feel comfortable with data stored remotely, it is a very wise step.

Planning for a disaster now will keep you out of crisis mode if or when one occurs. The more you plan now, the easier it will be for you to get back to business later. No one wants a disaster, but being prepared for one is critical to your company, your staff, your customers and you. You owe it to everyone to have a practical disaster plan in place, with copies stored in several locations so a single event can't wipe out your planning.

Chapter 8 - Chapter Wrap-Up

In this chapter you have learned:

- The Four Steps to Change Management are:

  1. Write down your plan.

  2. What you can describe, you can conquer.

  3. Make mid-course corrections frequently.

  4. Get help when you can't figure out a situation by yourself.

- Watch for and know about market changes.

- Watch and know your competition.

- Watch for grapevine rumors in the office. They include: Wish fulfillment, Bogey rumors, Wedge-drivers, and Home-stretchers.

- Keeping employees informed of business changes is helpful in preventing worrisome rumors from forming and circulating.

- Stay current with technology, but don't buy anything you don't need or won't profit from.

- You should strive for at least forty hours a year, for continuing education for yourself to keep you and your business at its highest potential.

- Stay up-to-date with all federal laws regarding your business. You should check the laws at least annually for any amendments, additions, or deletions.

- Prepare for natural disasters that happen not only in your area, but in the areas of your suppliers.

Chapter 8 - Summary Questions

 PDF's of these forms are available online at:
www.osteryoungobrien.com

Does your business fit into today's market place? _____

If so, how do you plan to maintain this position? _____

If not, what is your plan for change? _____
_____
_____

◆   ◆   ◆

Who is your competition? _____

What do they offer that you don't? _____

Is this a critical point to address? Why or why not? _____
_____
_____

*What is your plan to stay ahead of your competition?*_____
_____
_____

◆   ◆   ◆

*Do you currently keep your employees informed about company change?*_____

*How do you do this?*_____

If you don't - do you plan to start? _____

If so, when and how? _____
_____

Chapter 8 - Summary Questions

Review your current technology. Is it up-to-date? _____

*Would you benefit from an update?*_____

If yes, what do you need and why? If you don't know, ask an employee using the technology while reminding them of want vs. need. _____
_____
_____

Are the new technology items something you feel comfortable purchasing on your own? _____

*Have you done research on the items?*_____

Do you need to bring an employee or outside help in for the ordering/ purchasing process? _____

◆　　　◆　　　◆

*What is your current plan or procedure for on-going training and education for your employees as well as yourself?*_____
_____
_____

◆　　　◆　　　◆

How many employees do you have? _____

Are you currently up-to-date on the particular federal laws regarding the number of employees you have? _____

Do you know all the most recent forms you and your employees must legally fill out? _____

Chapter 8 - Summary Questions

Are you familiar with the newest minimum-wage requirements? ___

_____

Are you familiar with the newest discrimination laws? _____

◆　　　◆　　　◆

What is your disaster plan? _____

_____

_____

When was the last update? _____

Are you OSHA compliant? _____

Where do you back up your personal business files? Is this the safest place? _____

What do you have backed up? Is it current? When was the last time you verified it worked? _____

Does your disaster plan allow for your employees time to safely protect their own valuables and remove themselves from danger? __

Is your property adequately insured? _____

Is your coverage enough to really get you back up and running the way you are now? _____

Do you need to update your policy or increase your coverage limit? _

_____

Do you need to update your inventory list? _____

Chapter 8 – Take-Aways & Action Steps

Take-Aways and Action Steps

1. _____
_____
Completion Date: _____
*Results:*_____
_____

2. _____
_____
Completion Date: _____
*Results:*_____
_____

3. _____
_____
Completion Date: _____
*Results:*_____
_____

4. _____
_____
Completion Date: _____
*Results:*_____
_____

5. _____
_____
Completion Date: _____
*Results:*_____
_____

Chapter 9

Stress Management & Employee Wellness

●●●●●●●●●●●●●●●●●●●●●●●●●●●●●●●●●●●●

Chapter At-A-Glance

By the end of this chapter you will know:
- How to have fun at work and why it is important.

- How to avoid accidents in the workplace.

- What a corporate wellness plan is and why you should have one.

- How and why to set up a Drug-Free Work Place.

- How and why to set up a Smoke-Free Policy.

- How and why it is important to help your staff reduce the effects of stress.

Our main defense against disease is to not get sick. That's obvious, but in our fast-paced world that can be a tricky assignment. Unexpected deadlines or emotional shocks might deal the last blow needed to push our immune system into a weakened condition.

Our stress levels have a great impact on our overall health. The problem with stress arises from its unrelenting nature. The constant exposure, real or imagined, to anxiety and pressure weakens our immune system and makes us susceptible to disease. Under non-stressful conditions, our bodies have the resources to fight these diseases. However, with a diminished or impaired immune response system, we become vulnerable.

So, what do we do when we become ill? How do we heal ourselves while remaining in the same environment that contributed to our sickness? In some instances, we can't. In those instances, we must remove ourselves from our regular routine and simply recuperate. Another consideration is the health of others, our co-workers and employees. It is unfair to come into work when truly sick and possibly infect others. It is wise to allot three to five sick days into your overhead costs. Encourage employees to use them when truly sick. Discourage or penalize associates if they abuse the intent and use the sick days as "mental health days."

Many employees, business owners, and managers do not consider time off an option. When they experience a cold, the flu, or other uncomfortable but not immobilizing discomforts, they simply forge ahead, despite feeling miserable. Why? Cash flow, commitments, responsibilities, and a feeling of being indispensable keep people trudging on. Our plans, goals, and schedules seldom hold an entry for "sick time." We decide it is better to push ahead. Sometimes this effort is valiant; other times, it's just plain dumb.

It's impossible to guarantee that neither you nor your employees will ever become ill or have an accident. However, there are definite steps you can implement to slant the odds in your favor.

> ### Power Quote!
>
> *Encourage your employees to take a few short "brain breaks" every day. I call them "60-second sabbaticals."*
>
> *Stop and remember a favorite event or picture. Hum or sing a favorite tune. Go to the bathroom or get a drink of water.*
>
> **Tim O'Brien**

Healthy Fun

One of the simplest ways to improve the morale and health of your staff is to have fun around the office. Post inspirational and funny materials. Most of the time, workers tend towards the serious – it's rare to hear a laugh. Despite this, fun is one of the most basic human needs and laughter, especially, strengthens the immune system.

Accidents

When it comes to accidents, you need make your workplace as safe as practical. Accidents waiting to happen, from electrical cords on the floor to sharp desk corners, abound in both factory and office settings. Quite often, business owners or managers do not even recognize the hazards.

Liberty Mutual estimates that workplace injuries in our country exceed $50 billion dollars annually.

Some of the most common work place injuries are:

- *Overexertion*
- *Excessive lifting, pushing, pulling, holding, carrying, or throwing of an object*
- *Slipping, tripping, or falling*
- *Striking or being struck by an object*

While injuries occur in all workplaces, small business employees seem to be much more vulnerable. Big businesses have sufficient resources to evaluate safety issues and establish in-house safety programs; small businesses often do not. In addition, the cost of injuries can be much more devastating to small businesses. Between productivity losses due to injuries, increases in workman's compensation, premiums, and potential civil liabilities, small businesses may not have the income to cover the resulting expenses.

In addition to conducting a basic safety course for your company, you might also consider offering a wellness program for your employees. Encourage them to exercise aerobically at least three times a week for twenty minutes and to pump a little iron to boost both strength and bone density. As with any recommendations to exercise, always begin with the strong suggestion that participants consult their doctor before beginning any new or increased exercise routine to make sure it is appropriate for them.

Many gyms and health clubs offer reduced corporate rates. Assess whether you can afford to pay for a significant portion of membership costs. Fitter employees are healthier and more alert employees. And, remember to attend to your own exercise program.

S.A.F.E Exercises

Dr. Kenneth Cooper of the Aerobics Institute in Dallas, Texas, and the person who coined the word "aerobics," meaning "with oxygen," suggests that a full and effective exercise program will include strength, aerobic, and flexibility exercises. *Remember this acronym:*

S.A.F.E.= **S**trength, **A**erobic and **F**lexibility **E**xercises.

Hazardous Substances

Be careful with unknown substances. A basic radon check of your office costs about $35. You can find "do-it-yourself" kits at hardware and drug stores. If you notice your employees experiencing unusual health symptoms at the office, investigate. Don't be an alarmist, but do some detective work if everyone begins exhibiting similar symptoms only in certain areas of your office.

Drugs

The National Institute of Drug Addiction reports that substance abusers function at only sixty-seven percent of their capacity, drugs are involved in 3.6 times more accidents than non-drug users. According to the US Chamber of Commerce, employees using drugs are three times more likely to be late for work and 2.5 times more likely to have annual absences totalling eight or more days. The National Institute of Drug Addiction also reports that nearly ten percent of all employees use drugs in the workplace. The US Department of Justice shows that drug users are five times more likely to file a workers' compensation claim.

Online Resources

Company Fitness

Check out this fitness related web site set up by the President of the United States:

www.presidentschallenge.org/corporate/encourage.aspx.

This web site has many tips for helping you set up a physical fitness program for your business.

Drug-Free Workplace

The Small Business Administration has made funding available for business owners or managers to set up DFWP's in their businesses. You can find information on this program at:

http://www.sba.gov/index.html

Chapter 9 – Drugs

Those are scary statistics. As a business owner, you cannot put your head in the sand and pretend the drug problem does not exist. You might have been lucky so far in your company, however, drug abuse is a systemic problem within our society and the possibility exists that you will face it eventually. The courts have consistently upheld drug testing as a legitimate means of determining employees' ability to work. *Additionally, the courts have held that businesses are liable for accidents caused by employees using drugs when the company does not have a formal drug policy.* Read that last line again. If you don't have a formal drug policy in place or, you don't properly enforce the policy you do have, then you are liable for drug-related accidents at your company.

One of the best ways to deter drug use is to adopt a drug-free work place policy (DFWP) which should contain the following three basic elements:

1. *A written policy.*
2. *Mandatory staff training.*
3. *Mandatory drug testing*

Most firms test employees for drugs pre-employment, post-accident, and when they return to work after an accident. In addition, many firms administer drug tests at random throughout the year. If you think this sounds expensive, consider the potential liability costs of inaction. You might find the costs of implementing a plan is at least partially offset by premium savings. Check with your insurance carrier; many companies offer premium discounts to firms that enact a DWFP program.

Smoking

While many factors contribute to a first impression of your business, public smoking by your employees will assuredly destroy it. Customers who see, or smell, a group of smokers hovering on your property, create a negative impression of your company. Consider banning smoking at your office, both for your public image and for your associates' health.

The harmful health effects of smoking and secondhand smoke are common knowledge. To address this concern, there are three potential solutions.

1. Ban smoking, dipping or chewing of tobacco products on your premises entirely: inside, outside or anywhere on your property.

This action is a strong statement of your belief in a healthy workforce. Other ways to manage the issue without an all-out ban:

Cancer

The American Cancer Society website has many good resources and support materials for business owners, including guidelines for setting up a smoke-free workplace and pre-written policy statements.
www.cancer.org

2. Designate a smoking area that is out of view of the customer, certainly away from any doors a potential client, customer or investor might use.

3. Consider including a smoking cessation program in your comprehensive wellness program.

A smoking cessation program is not a standalone solution; it should be coupled with one of the other two options.

Chapter 9 – Stress Management Techniques

Five Stress Management Techniques

Each of the following techniques takes less than one minute. Try them all. Then, choose the two or three that give you the most relief and relaxation. Begin to use them several times per day, every day, when you find yourself in a stressful situation:

1 **Stop your current activity.** Take long, slow, deep breaths allowing your stomach to expand and contract. Blink your eyes as you breathe. Feel the coolness of the air as it enters through your nose. Feel the warmth of the air as it leaves through your nose.

2 **Sit up straight. Close your eyes.** Lift your shoulders up toward your ears. Roll them in exaggerated circles toward the back three times. Now, change directions and roll them in three large circles toward the front. Breathe deeply, calmly, as you roll your shoulders. Finally, raise your shoulders up toward your ears and then drop them by releasing all muscle tension. Do this three times. Take one final deep breath and go back to work.

3 **Break your concentration,** especially when you feel stuck or frustrated. Get up. Walk around your office, or get a drink at the water fountain. When you go back to the work, sit in a different chair. Turn on a different light. Use a different pen. Change small details surrounding the situation frustrating you.

4 **Close your eyes and remember** a fun, beautiful, or exciting situation from the past. See the sights. Smell the smells. Hear the sounds. Imagine the textures. Enter into this as vividly as your can. Breathe deeply, calmly, as you recall this event. Enjoy it.

5 **Wiggle your toes.** This one sounds odd, however, it offers a very pleasant, tingling sensation. Concentrate on your toes and the feelings created. Take off your shoes if appropriate. Keep wiggling. It will make you smile in less than 60 seconds.

These stress relievers will help you if you remember to use them regularly and often. Get into the habit of doing one technique each hour and you will find that both your energy and concentration levels improve.

Stress

Stress can be caused by any change in your normal routine. Stress happens when good things happen, as well as when bad things occur. When the body experiences stress, it goes into overdrive and is ready for the "fight-or-flight" response cavemen exhibited to survive attacks from wild animals. The body's reaction to stress, whether actual or perceived, is to produce a hormone called cortisol. Its function is to rev the body up to deal with the stressful event. Our body was engineered to deal with stressful situations (being chased by a lion) and then to move on to something without stress (strolling in a meadow).

However, in the workplace we cannot always express and release the stress we're under. Yelling at the boss or customers is just not acceptable. Also, we do not have many stress-free hours during the day. Therefore, instead of letting stress go, people tend to experience a buildup. Stress has become

Sleep

- Sleep is nature's ultimate stress management tool.
- Sleep naturally without aids, like alcohol or drugs. They can induce sleep but they can't induce rest.
- Have a nightly ritual that helps you prepare for sleep.

Meditation

- Meditation is the process of stopping the thinking process.
- When your mind is thought-free it is relaxed and peaceful.
- Meditation gives many benefits and is easy to learn.

www.hyperstress.com/meditation

long-term in nature.

The problem is that this effects the health of your workers. Some of the problems that typically manifest themselves as a result of stress are depression, emotional fatigue, headaches, and boredom. The effects can also be seen in high staff turnover, increased absenteeism, and reduced work performance. Stress also affects those who cover for their stressed colleague(s).

One common way to deal with stress in the workplace is to teach your employees to manage their time better, as much stress arises from feeling incapable of meeting others' expectations. Another solution is to offer employees some extra vacation time to allow a break from the cycle of stress. Two weeks of continuous vacation

Grief Stress

The loss of a spouse or loved one is the most severe stress inducer a person can experience. On the Holmes-Rahe Scale of leading stressors it is #1.

Our society does not have a formal grieving ritual like many other countries do. And, people often feel that those who "can't get over it and get on with it," are weak.

When you or an employee suffers the loss of a special person, be compassionate, sensitive and understanding in dealing with their missed days and probable low productivity levels. Don't make employees bring in the program from the funeral to prove they cared. (This has happened!)

Everyone experiences grief differently. There is no magic timetable for the grieving process. While there are common stages of grief, the frequency, duration, and intensity of the episodes and stages are unique to each person.

www.hyperstress.com/grief

is more effective at reducing stress than two, one-week vacations.

Another valuable suggestion for you and your employees is to encourage physical exercise. Research shows that regular exercise releases stress, improves the immune system and increases mental alertness. Exercise should be a major cornerstone in everyone's personal stress management program, including, and perhaps most importantly, for business

Dealing with Stress

Here is the progression for dealing with stress:

- **Admit it.** When a situation cannot be changed quickly, or perhaps at all, admit this to your employee.
- **Accept it.** Don't waste positive energy resisting the obvious or the inevitable.
- **Learn to enjoy it.** Work to modify stress by ensuring that your associate's tasks incorporate the elements of success: a defined challenge that the employee accepts, identifiable rules that govern behavior toward the challenge, specific goals that lead to mastery of the challenge, and constant, consistent feedback that allows your associate to know their rate of progress.
- **Maintain control.** Even if the situation cannot be changed, the way that individuals react to it can be controlled. Have clear behavioral guidelines set for yourself and your employees. Stick to them.
- **Leave.** If you work through the previous suggestions and the situation does not improve, consider letting the employee go. This is a serious step with serious implications. However, you must maturely consider the options and alternatives against the consequences of continuing the present course. This is a drastic step. Take it judiciously.

owners. If you die or become incapacitated prematurely, it impacts everyone.

Some companies offer stress reduction workshops. These workshops can give employees the tools they need to deal with stress. If you offer stress management programs be sure to have a system of reminders and support in place to ensure the benefits from the stress management training last beyond the day of the seminar.

Stress, especially excessive stress (which results in burnout), affects both the

Types of Stress

Our Autonomic Nervous System (ANS) has two parts: **the sympathetic system** and the **parasympathetic system**. Although most people associate stress with sympathetic, *"fight-or-flight,"* responses, parasympathetic, *"freeze from fright,"* responses can be equally harmful.

Sympathetic System

The mild response:
These are life's little annoyances and habituated behaviors that keep us "wound up," anything that stimulates us regularly or for a prolonged period, either consciously or unconsciously.

The severe response:
Anger, hostility and aggression and any other extreme example of the "fight-or-flight," response.

Parasympathetic System

The mild response:
Repetitious, monotonous activities cause our bodies to begin to shut down. Boring lectures, sitting for long periods and conditioned, dulling responses fit here.

The severe response:
Depression, seasonal affective disorder (SAD), and responses of extreme withdrawal are a total dominant reaction by the parasympathetic half of the ANS.

mental and physical health of your workers. If you see your workers under a lot of stress, you need to find a way to reduce their load. Otherwise it will lead to burnout, and you will lose valuable employees. Great management requires monitoring the stress levels of your staff and then taking action to ensure they do not become overwhelmed. While there are times when "burning the candle at both ends" can't be avoided, if these times occur frequently in your company, something is wrong.

Presenteeism

"Presenteeism" is a newly coined word referring to the loss of productivity resulting from a worker showing up to work but who is not fully engaged.

Power Quote!

"Employers worry a lot about absenteeism, but new research suggests a bigger threat to productivity is "presenteeism": sick workers who show up at work but are not fully functioning. U.S. companies may lose $150 billion (yes, that's billion) annually because of presenteeism, according to some estimates."
- Harvard Business Review

Whether due to illness, distraction, burnout or depression, presenteeism amounts to workers who are physically present, but mentally elsewhere.

According to one study, the loss in productivity from employees who came to work while ill was significantly higher than in those who were absent.

When employees go to work ill, it tends to affect the entire workforce. Nearly $100,000 in labor costs could have been saved at this company had sick employees just stayed home.

One of the most common ways to address presenteeism is by instituting a corporate wellness program. These programs are designed to help employees stay healthy through both treatment and education. You can also reduce the amount of presenteeism by offering paid sick leave and allowing that sick leave to carry over from one year to the next. Additionally, helping the employee cover their physician co-payments encourages them to go to the doctor when they are not feeling well. You also might consider helping them cover some of their prescription costs. For example, flu shots should be provided free-of-charge as not providing them can have a major impact on the entire business.

■ Corporate Wellness Program ■

According to the U.S. Government, adults are considered to be physically active if they engage in at least thirty minutes of moderate physical activities at least five days a week. The majority of our workforce is just not that physically active. Sitting at a desk all day does not generate the requisite amount of activity necessary for health and productivity.

Obesity, according to WebMD.com, is an excess of body weight totaling twenty percent or more above normal

Calories In & Out

- Calories ingested vs. calories burned determines if we gain weight, lose weight, or maintain our weight.
- If we burn more calories than we eat, we lose. If we eat more than we burn, we gain. It's that simple.
- Education, exercise, and self control are the keys to maintaining an ideal body weight.

body weight. In the United States, obesity is a growing trend. In 2005, the CDC stated thirty-four percent of U.S. adults aged twenty and over were obese. Obesity cuts across all ages, races, and genders.

Chapter 9 – Encouragement

Diabetes increased from 5.8 million in 1980 to 17.9 million diagnosed cases in 2007 according to the American Diabetes Association.

As an entrepreneur, you are concerned with preventive maintenance of your equipment. You know maintaining it will allow it to last longer and work more effectively. A corporate wellness program is analogous to preventive maintenance.

Encouragement

Some simple actions you can take to improve your workers' health:

- Bring guest speakers to your staff meetings. Nutritionists, personal trainers, and relaxation therapists can educate and motivate your staff.

- Negotiate lower rates at various fitness facilities for your staff and possibly reimburse employees for some of their fitness expenses.

- Encourage employees to get involved in sports activities and support them by being flexible with their work schedules.

- Ask your workers which health programs they would like to adopt for staff participation. This is a wonderful way to acquire employee buy-in to this new emphasis.

- Make a point of encouraging physical fitness in your organization. Start with yourself, then encourage your employees to follow your example. The more physically fit your business is, the better your business will likely be.

- Have a wellness committee that educates and encourages everyone, company wide. Don't let them go overboard, but monthly updates and suggestions and a few motivational posters are a good idea. Be positive openly, negative subtly.

Chapter 9 – The First Symptom

The First Symptom

Forty percent of all people affected by coronary heart disease result in **sudden death.**

Sudden death is defined as **death within 24 hours** of the onset of symptoms.

We can't recover from sudden death so it is very important to develop and maintain a healthy lifestyle.

A corporate wellness program is generally started by assessing your firm's employees' real needs. The health of your workforce may be measured by fitness testing, blood work to check cholesterol and glucose, and smoking and substance abuse surveys. Of course, all the information gathered in testing like this must remain confidential and cannot be released to anyone but the employee. Normally, the firm receives a summary document that shows the overall health of their workforce, but no specific information on individual employees. These assessments normally cost less than $100 per employee.

Once you know your workforce's overall state of health, the next step is devising a plan to instigate healthier lifestyle habits. Some firms fund payment for health club memberships, massages (for stress reduction), for classes to improve health awareness and for smoking/other addictive substance cessation programs.

As with other plans directly involving your employees, it is helpful to solicit staff involvement as early as possible. Get the staff to help analyze results. Let them make recommendations for the program based on a proposed budget. The more help you have from your workforce in devising the plan, the more successful it should be.

Business owners and managers spend many hours planning how to improve their businesses. One aspect often neglected is their own health and the health of their workers.

Chapter 9 – Mastering Time

7 Steps to Mastering Time

For a poster with more details on the 7 Steps to Mastering Time visit:

www.hyperstress.com/timemanagement

- **Setting Priorities and Goals**
  Think of priorities and goals as a road map; your priority is your destination, goals are how you get there.

- **Estimating Time Requirements**
  You'll work best if you assign time frames to your activities. Initially it will be more art than science, but as you gain experience your guesses will evolve into accurate estimations.

- **Allocating Your Day**
  Write out your seven goals for tomorrow. Next to each entry, write how much time you'll spend on each one.

- **Touch it once, do it now, do it right the first time.**
  Do quality work as you go. Don't put off a project or task unless absolutely necessary. Do it now!

- **Consolidate and Simplify**
  First, decide on one major accomplishment for the month. Then, decide what two actions to accomplish each week to reach the goal. Finally, break down your week into three daily tasks to complete.

- **Tackling the Tough Tasks**
  We all have tough and unpleasant tasks. Don't let them take control! Do your most important work first.

- **Just One More Task**
  Many experts recommend scheduling six tasks a day. After completing them, choose one more important, but not pressing task, or an unpleasant one & do it.

Chapter 9 – Corporate Wellness Program

The return on spending just a little bit of money can be very high in terms of productivity. Concern over health and fitness also shows your staff that you value them.

Some business owners and managers may say that what their workers do outside of the workplace is none of the employer's business. However, what your workers do outside the workplace has a dramatic impact on how they respond in the workplace. Investing even a small amount of money on a staff wellness program often pays significant dividends. The return on this type of investment will be very high in regards to reduced absenteeism, lower health care costs, higher productivity, and increased employee satisfaction.

Chapter Wrap-Up

Chapter Wrap-Up

In this chapter you have learned:

- Laughter and fun strengthen the immune system. Encourage fun in the workplace.

- Some of the most common workplace injuries are:

  o overexertion

  o excessive lifting, pushing, pulling, holding, carrying or throwing of an object

  o slipping, tripping or falling

  o striking or being struck by an object

- Get as much employee feedback and involvement as possible when planning your corporate wellness plan.

- If an employee is ill, it is more cost effective for them to stay home and visit a doctor, if needed.

- Benefits for having a corporate wellness plan include:

  o Reduced absenteeism

  o Lower health care costs

  o Higher productivity

  o Increased employee satisfaction

Continued Next Page

Chapter Wrap-Up Continued

- You need a written policy, staff training, and drug testing to set up a drug-free work place.

- To have a smoke-free workplace you must ban all inside tobacco use entirely, designate a tobacco use area out of sight and smell range, and start a tobacco cessation program.

- A few ways to eliminate employee stress are time management, extra vacation time, and stress reduction workshops.

- The progression for dealing with stress is:

  o Admit it

  o Accept it

  o Learn to enjoy it

  o Maintain control

  o Leave

FYI! PDF's of these forms are available online at:
www.osteryoungobrien.com
enter code: OST+OBR=2010

▬ The BREADS Formula ▬

*The 12 parts of a complete **S**tress **M**anagement **A**nd **R**elaxation **T**echniques (S.M.A.R.T.) Program*

In 1990, The Institute for Stress Management & Performance Improvement introduced its five step **BREAD** formula for effective stress management. In recent years, medical and psychological research has discovered new relationships for managing stress. So, the Institute revised its **BREAD** formula to a twelve steps **BREADS** formula, to reflect these mind/body relationships. *www.hyperstress.com/stressrelief*

PSYCHOLOGICAL		PHYSIOLOGICAL
Belief System Those with strong faith are more resilient.	**B**	**Breath** Breathe calmly, with your diaphragm.
Relationships A strong social support system adds to life.	**R**	**Relaxation** Take regular breaks: hourly, daily, monthly, & yearly.
Education Learn new skills; practice what you learn.	**E**	**Exercise often** (Strength, Flexibility, Aerobic, Exercises) Remember S.A.F.E.
Attitude Be positive! Optimists live longer.	**A**	**Activity** Walk, bend, stretch, play. Keep active everyday.
Determination Stay committed to your plan. Never give up.	**D**	**Diet** We really are what we eat. Study nutrition; eat well.
Serenity Practice having internal peace and calmness of mind.	**S**	**Sleep** Adequate natural sleep is nature's #1 restorative power.

169

Use the checklist of suggestions from this chapter to help you and your employees create a corporate wellness program.

☐ Improve company morale by having productive fun around the office.

☐ Encourage "Brain Breaks," short "60 second sabbaticals."

☐ Check your office and correct any "Accidents Waiting to Happen."

☐ Practice the S.A.F.E. technique for exercising.

☐ Check your office for hazardous materials.

☐ Implement drug testing with a DFWP program.

☐ Implement a smoking policy.

☐ Try the 5 Stress Management Techniques. See which ones work best for you. Share them with your employees.

☐ Teach employees to manage their time at work better.

☐ Offer extra vacation time if your employees are overstressed.

☐ Encourage physical activity.

☐ Offer stress reduction workshops.

Chapter 9 – Chapter Checklist

☐ Find ways to reduce heavy workloads so employees don't feel overwhelmed.

☐ Encourage employees to stay home if ill and to go to see a doctor if necessary.

☐ Offer paid sick leave that can carry over each month or year if not used.

☐ If possible, help with co-payments, prescriptions, or checkups. Offer company-wide flu shots.

☐ Bring in guest speakers such as nutritionists, personal trainers, and relaxation therapists.

☐ Use the B.R.E.A.D.S. Formula to develop your personal S.M.A.R.T. program.

Wellness Resource

For a good resource with information about starting a Corporate Wellness Program, visit the Wellness Council of America's website at:

http://www.welcoa.org

FYI! PDF's of these forms are available online at:
www.osteryoungobrien.com
enter code: **OST+OBR=2010**

Chapter 9 – Take-Aways & Action Steps

Take-Aways and Action Steps

1. _____

_____

Completion Date: _____

Results:_____

_____

2. _____

_____

Completion Date: _____

Results:_____

_____

3. _____

_____

Completion Date: _____

Results:_____

_____

4. _____

_____

Completion Date: _____

Results:_____

_____

5. _____

_____

Completion Date: _____

Results:_____

_____

Chapter 10
Team Building
• •

Chapter At-A-Glance

By the end of this chapter you will know:

- Why teamwork is vital to a successful business.

- Why it is important to develop a question-and-action checklist before starting a team project.

- Why it is important to have a Code of Behavior.

- The differences between audio, visual, and kinesthetic communications.

- How to recognize and correct employee conflicts.

- What T.E.A.M. means and how to build team trust.

Creating teamwork in a business is not much different than managing an athletic team. In both cases, each team member should be managed so they understand their boss is 100% behind them.

Continually tend to the priorities and goals of the total business and team. Employees tend to speculate about the new idea or plan for "this" month. When you commit to developing teamwork in your business, you must do it full-time, all the time, there are no "off days." If you focus in on team building, your business will function much more smoothly and you will find that you have to spend less time dealing with employee problems.

One of the most critical steps in teamwork is developing trust between employees. It is very hard for an employee to willingly help the team grow and prosper if they do not trust their team members. How distrust entered in is immaterial; what is important is to build trust so everyone is willing to risk some of him or herself to contribute to the team.

Managing Teams

Make sure you learn from your past experiences with each member on the team. Don't assume your employees will not repeat mistakes. While you certainly don't want to become paranoid, assuming your employee's previous slip was a simple mistake may be inaccurate. The issue may have been caused by a deeper misunderstanding. **Adjust your caution and your response to the stakes involved in each project.**

Preemptively act in situations where you or others have made assumptions in the past which caused problems. Before the group begins a project, subject it to a thorough review process. Consider the following questions during your review. Where have

> ### Power Quote!
>
> *"If we are going to have a great team, we need to make sure we select great team members."*
>
> **- Jerry Osteryoung**

there been problems with this project, or similar projects in the past? Are there people involved in this project who have made erroneous assumptions before? What aspects of the project are the most familiar to everyone? Which are the most complex? Which parts are most likely to cause problems?

Familiarity promotes laxity. The more familiar a person, system or project is, the easier it is for the people involved to make assumptions which may be inaccurate.

Set up safeguards to prevent assuming. Have team members write out questions or develop a checklist. Break familiar, critical tasks down into individual components. Then, implement a double check-off system to counter the urge to check items off cavalierly. Have sign-offs and counter sign-off procedures in place.

It is impossible to completely stop assumptions. In fact, if we didn't take certain activities and people for granted, we'd accomplish very little. There are places to guard diligently against assuming, though. When you assign a project to a team, don't assume that your employees fully understand the scope and importance of the project. When you present your employees with a new project, ask them to explain to you what they understand the project to encompass. Then require status reports on an appropriately frequent timetable. This will help you ensure the project progresses properly and on schedule. Make benchmarks and measures part of your review and assessment process for the project. Develop a realistic timetable for the project so everyone knows, with a simple glance at a calendar if they are on or off schedule.

Group Dynamics

Ritualized behavior is a part of all cohesive groups. Most ritual behavior pertains to mundane duties, not glory filled ones, but ones that are generally accepted. Some acts are serious or obviously necessary, others sublimely ridiculous. In one team, it may become a ritual for one member to bring coffee or bagels on a Saturday morning. In another, there may be a certain member who is always in charge of taking notes. There are power and stature rituals. There are "low-person-on-the-pole" rituals. Sometimes, these rituals cause laughter and harmony. At other times, they

Chapter 10 – Audio, Visual, & Kinesthetic

Audio, Visual, & Kinesthetic

Communication is a vital aspect of team dynamics. Often, though, it seems impossible for group members to communicate effectively. It's almost as though they're speaking different languages.

"Why can't you two see what I'm saying?"
"It's not us, Jim; you just don't hear what Tom's telling you."
"Hold on. I really believe that we just haven't grasped the concept as a team yet. Let's walk through it again from the beginning, OK?"

Each of the three persons involved in the above dialogue has a different primary way of relating to the world. As humans, we often incorrectly surmise that we all experience the world in the same way. This is the fallacy of self projection. It leads us to believe that, when others don't understand us, they are somehow less intelligent than we are. In fact, it might be our own ignorance that creates the problem.

There are three primary ways of relating to the world:

Visual (seeing)
The first person relates visually: "Can't you *see* what I'm saying?"

Audio (hearing)
The second person is auditory: "You don't *hear*."

Kinesthetic (touching)
The third person relates kinesthetically with three touching references: "*Hold* on...*grasped* the concept...let's *walk* through it."

When we as individuals first identify what our primary way of relating to the world is and then develop the ability to assess another's way of relating, we can learn to adjust our conversational style to fit the situation. We can learn to speak someone else's language and translate it into ours.

may create discord. Regardless, rituals are a required part of human dynamics.

Rituals help to define accepted and assigned roles. When these assigned roles are perceived as acceptable and fair, the group prospers. The rituals can give the group energy and promote long-term continuity. Conscious rituals can improve the quality of group dynamics and help those involved remember all required steps of intricate or detailed activities.

There is also a negative side to ritualized behavior. Behaviors that benefit only a few or foster bigotry and bias will destroy team dynamics. It's important to pay attention to what behaviors are common in each team and deal with issues before they cause serious problems. Unconscious ritual is unconscious habit and as such, doesn't have intrinsic worth. Bad rituals need to be eliminated, while the good ones that foster community spirit and trust between team members are retained. It is the latter which will enhance productivity and morale.

When people function on autopilot, the term "no-brainer" applies. Be careful. Every team, every business, has both written and implied codes of behavior. They define acceptable and unacceptable rituals for the group. For individuals and groups that are growth and improvement-oriented, these codes can become antiquated. It is a good idea to set up periodic reviews for the written codes and goals of your business.

Work to ensure that

T.E.A.M.

T.E.A.M. = Together, Everyone Accomplishes More

This implies synergy, cooperation, collective and productive effort.

Use posters, quotes and other devices to help your employees develop a sense of mutual support (not dependence).

your corporate code of behavior evolves with your company, its needs, and the needs of your employees. This is not a suggestion to take Machiavellian license and do whatever is expedient in the moment. It does mean adjust codes to fit the style and language of the time and circumstance. Have a written code of acceptable behavior. Make certain that the language used is as clear to an octogenarian as it is to a teenager, and to each culture involved. Ensure that it is followed.

Having clear-cut guidelines for behavior and individual roles helps eliminate uncertainty. The better your employees understand what is expected of them, the better they are at delivering it.

Employee Conflicts

Bad Apples

"One bad apple can spoil the whole bunch."

This is an old but wise cliché.

- A negative, sarcastic, critical employee can create a miserable work environment faster than almost anything else.
- Don't allow one or two negative employees to ruin your "fun workplace" for everyone.
- This can be a touchy topic. Be careful how you handle it. If you have a problem, admit it and deal with it quickly.

There are really two points you must keep in mind when dealing with team members who are not getting along. The first point is to be alert, so you recognize the symptoms of problems very early. Problems normally don't suddenly erupt into all-out hostility. Rather, it is usually a slow simmer that gradually builds. The second critical element is to know how to deal with the problem once you recognize it. You

Chapter 10 – Angels & Peacemakers

must deal with the problem, because unresolved problems will affect the entire workplace. Employee conflicts only get worse unattended.

Recognizing conflict is key, because it is impossible to take action unless you know there is a problem. A sure warning sign for potential conflict is when it is well known that two employees just do not like one another. When employees are overheard taking sides with various other employees, there exists the probability for conflict. If a staff member approaches you for a solution, you know the situation has become serious.

A sudden change in an employee's workplace behavior might also signal potential conflict. For example, if a previously dedicated employee started coming in late or missing work on a frequent basis, you may want to question him or her about the cause of the problem. It could very well be a conflict with another employee.

Angels & Peacemakers

Often overlooked and certainly under appreciated are your employees who act as angels and peacemakers.

Thank and show appreciation to your angels and peacemakers in their respective styles.

Angels work quietly, more often one-on-one. They try to quietly solve problems they believe can disrupt everyone.

Before acknowledging angels publicly, talk privately and quietly with them to get their permission.

Peacemakers are natural arbitrators who try to get opposing views reconciled for the good of the group. They will work more openly than angels.

You can discuss more openly with your peacemakers concerning how they'd like public praise handled.

Chapter 10 – An In-House Court?

Once you identify a problem, you must take action. The first step should be to address the employees, separately to discern the real issues. If the problem is not solved during individual interviews, meet with the employees jointly. Guard your credibility by refusing to place blame or take sides. Address the specifics of the situation rather than talking in generalities. Identify both the specific problem and specific solutions to remedy it.

When talking individually, you must acknowledge the conflict exists. Words such as, "Sally, I understand that you and Gayle are not getting along," usually bring everything out into the open. Once this has been done, you need to explain to your employees how their conflict is affecting the entire organization, giving specific examples. Finally, mention the consequences of failing to resolve the conflict, making sure your employees clearly understand your intention to follow through. If talking to them individually does not

An In-House Court?

If you have some long term, well-respected employees. Consider allowing them to set up an "in-house court system," for internal conflicts that won't go away.

Have specific guidelines on "the court's" powers. Often, intelligent employees can come up with intelligent solutions.

solve the problem, the next step is bringing them together for a meeting.

Bringing both parties in for a discussion requires careful monitoring on your part, because it could easily get out of hand. Points both parties must agree on are that

1. *They do actually have a conflict.*
2. *In the future, they will not discuss the conflict with others at work.*
3. *Both employees understand what behaviors are acceptable in the workplace*

and which are not (e.g., making faces, asking other staff to take sides, or speaking in a disrespectful tone of voice).

If necessary, create an arbitration process (either formal or informal) to implement if and/or when these employees have problems in the future. Also, in this meeting, clearly convey how you will monitor their behavior to ensure the conflict is resolved, and delineate the specific consequences of noncompliance.

Trust-Building Ideas

How can entrepreneurs work with their associates to develop the trust so necessary for team building? One option you may want to consider is an outdoor, team building activity, such as a low ropes course. During this challenge, each team member learns how to trust their co-workers.

A similar exercise includes an exercise when one person falls backwards into the hands of his fellow workers who must catch him. Be careful! Only attempt these exercises under the guidance of trained professionals.

Another concept that works well in team building is

What is Trust?

If you can't answer the following questions, you have a problem.

- *What does trust mean to you?*
- *What does it mean to your employees?*
- *What does it mean to your vendors/suppliers?*
- *What does it mean to your customers and clients?*

Once you know the answer, determine whether you have a disconnect between any of these critical stakeholders?

Develop a **"Trust Statement."** Get input and buy-in from all key groups - AND yourself. Assume nothing! Trust is too important.

Chapter 10 – Dispersed Teams

Dispersed Teams

Here is an online resource for specific ideas to for building trust for teams that are spread out.

www.agora-business-center.com/0507teams.html

This is a 7-step process for building trust in dispersed teams. Today, with many businesses spread around the world, teams often consist of many sub-contractors mixed in with direct employees. Trust can be tricky in this case.

the "Star Approach" developed by Glen Davidson (CEO of PAT Live in Tallahassee, FL). With the Star Approach, each employee is given three stars a month. At the monthly company meetings, the employees present these stars to another employee who has made a difference in their job that month. One star must go to someone within the department and not the same person every month. The other two stars must go to people outside of the employee's department.

At the staff meeting, both the giver and recipient of the star stand. The employee giving the star reads what he or she has written on the front of the star describing how the other person has contributed.

After an employee receives a certain number of stars, they are eligible for company rewards. With this type of team building, each employee is recognizing other employees as critical team members.

Another way employees can build trust is through consistently doing what they have promised. When others know they can depend on a person to come through as promised, trust exists.

Holiday parties are super ways to encourage team building. At these festive events everyone can relax and get to know their coworkers in a non-stressful environment.

As you start to plan for the holidays, please consider making holiday functions alcohol-free. Many firms have changed from evening to luncheon events to avoid the alcohol issue. You want everyone to have a good time, but not at the cost of someone getting injured or worse. The potential for liability is not worth the risk. Also, many people act very differently when they've had a drink or two. You want the memories of the party to be happy ones, not remorseful.

Also, avoid hosting holiday events in your home. Inviting employees to your home may trigger envious feelings in your staff. You also invite the potential for theft. There are lines of separation that must be kept between staff and management. Avoiding social functions in your home is one way to keep your business and personal life separate.

Row in the same direction

Trust also develops or devolves through our everyday, mundane interactions with others. When we "get to know someone," we either develop a like or dislike for them. We are seldom ambivalent.

Encourage your employees to find out what they have in common and accentuate those features, while down-playing what they perceive as points of contention.

Consider hanging a poster in your break room reminding everyone you are all working toward the same goals.

You can download a free 11"x 17" poster on cooperation at:

www.hyperstress.com/cooperation

You'll find it both funny and effective in getting your point across.

Chapter Wrap-Up

Chapter Wrap-Up

In this chapter you have learned:

- Teamwork is a MUST for successful business.

- When a group is working on a project have them develop a question-and-action checklist. Perform a double-check system.

- Set up periodical review of the written conduct codes and company goals.

- The three modes of communication are Audio, Visual, and Kinesthetic.

- Deal with problems immediately - allowing them to go unresolved will affect the entire workplace.

- Consider adding team building exercises to your company's agenda.

- T.E.A.M. = **T**ogether, **E**veryone **A**ccomplishes **M**ore

FYI! PDF's of these forms are available online at:
www.osteryoungobrien.com
enter code: **OST+OBR=2010**

Chapter 10 – Business Goals & Projects

Giving the required attention to your business goals and projects on a regular basis is key to successful business. Before starting a project with a team of employees, make sure you answer the following questions to ensure smooth operations.

*What are your business goals?*_____

_____

*What are the steps necessary for achieving these goals?*_____

_____

What teams or project groups will you need for these goals? _____

_____

Who will be in the teams/groups? _____

_____

Where have there been problems with this project, or similar projects in the past? _____

_____

Are there people involved in this project who have made erroneous assumptions on previous projects? _____

*What aspects of the project are the most familiar to everyone?*_____

_____

Which are the most complex? _____

_____

Which are most likely to cause problems? _____

_____

Chapter 10 – Develop A Trust Statement

How often will you review the project status with your teams? _____

_____

How will you measure progress? _____

_____

Do you have or need a double check-off system for your team? If yes, who will oversee this? _____

_____

*Have you developed a timeline with benchmarks and deadlines?*___

_____

Does everyone have a copy clearly showing their team and individual responsibilities? _____

_____

Develop a Trust Statement. To help you with this, answer the following questions asked previously in the chapter. Discuss these questions with each group.

What does trust mean to you? _____

_____

What does it mean to your employees? _____

_____

What does it mean to vendors/suppliers? _____

_____

What does it mean to your customers and clients? _____

_____

Chapter 10 – Communication Style

Make a list of your employees. Next to each name write the communication style you believe they use (audio, visual, or kinesthetic). Use this information to help you communicate more effectively with each employee.

Employee   **Communication Style**

_____   _____

_____   _____

_____   _____

_____   _____

_____   _____

_____   _____

_____   _____

_____   _____

_____   _____

Chapter 10 – Employee Conflict

Deal with problems immediately; allowing them to go unresolved will affect the entire workplace. Before meeting with conflicting employees, devise a game plan. Know how you will handle the situation, the questions you will ask, and any associated consequences. Ask yourself the following questions:

What is your action plan for dealing with employee conflicts? _____

_____

What are the consequences of employee noncompliance? _____

_____

Company "angels and peacemakers" usually try to resolve conflicts between coworkers themselves.

Do you know who your "angels" are? _____

_____

Do you know who your "peacemakers" are? _____

_____

How do you acknowledge and show your "angels" appreciation? ___

_____

How do you acknowledge and show your "peacemakers" appreciation? _____

_____

Chapter 10 – Team Building

Team building events/exercises can play a big part in developing employee-team trust.

What trust building exercises do you have planned for your employees? _____

_____

_____

When/how often do you plan to have these events? _____

_____

_____

Will they be mandatory or voluntary? Why? _____

_____

_____

*If mandatory, how will you enforce it? What are the consequences for not attending and how will the employees be informed of this?*__

_____

_____

If voluntary and few, or no one, attends, how will you catch their interest next time? _____

_____

_____

 PDF's of these forms are available online at:
www.osteryoungobrien.com
enter code: **OST+OBR=2010**

Chapter 10 – Take-Aways & Action Steps

Take-Aways and Action Steps

1. _____

_____

Completion Date: _____

Results: _____

_____

2. _____

_____

Completion Date: _____

Results: _____

_____

3. _____

_____

Completion Date: _____

Results: _____

_____

4. _____

_____

Completion Date: _____

Results: _____

_____

5. _____

_____

Completion Date: _____

Results: _____

_____

Chapter 11

Communication & Task Saturation

Chapter At-A-Glance

By the end of this chapter you will know:

- How to tell if you are being clear with your employees, regarding what is expected of them.

- The "three one-minute secrets" and how to use them.

- Why to be aware of your body language.

- Task Saturation: What it means, how best to avoid it, and how to use the "4 D's."

- How to differentiate between loyalty and productivity.

- The Five Clarities and how to use them.

- How to tell if your company has an information blocker.

- Proper termination procedures.

Inefficient communications can lead to enormous problems. Offering criticism in a joking manner is a common mistake made by business owners and managers. Statements like, "If you spent more time working on XYZ project, my wife could buy furniture for our new house,"

Chapter 11 - One-Minute Techniques

One-Minute Techniques

When dealing with employees, especially problem employees, use Blanchard and Spencer's three "one-minute secrets."

1. One minute goals
2. One minute praise
3. One minute reprimand

Using these techniques forces you to be concise, precise, and direct.

Consider in advance what you will say at each step. Write it down. Speak with the employee, and come to an understanding. Make sure your agreement is put in written form.

Check the following link for a brief summary of their book, "The One Minute Manager."

www.bruinleaders.ucla.edu/documents/

BLP_samplebookreview.pdf

fail to convey a message. Any meaning is obscured because; there is no clear direction. If you give criticism in this manner, your corrections will not be taken seriously, as your employees will be unable to tell if you are sincere or joking. If you have to correct an employee, choose your words with care and then speak plainly.

One tip for improving your communications is to watch your pace. People assume that those who speak rapidly are agitated. Frequently, this sends a danger signal to the listener, which can interfere with the message. Experiment to see how others respond while you speak. If an employee appears to have difficulty following what you say, slow down. Repeat yourself, if necessary. If a staff member is nodding his head, it is a good indicator that your pace is appropriate and he understands the message.

Another point to remember about communications is that body language affects the message. Normally, messages sent with incongruent emotions are either completely misunderstood or not heard at all. For instance, we have seen managers compliment staff members while frowning and standing with very rigid posture. The message is received as aggression instead of as a compliment. Similarly, smiling while telling an employee she has a problem with her behavior, sends a mixed message.

Make sure that your message and emotions are congruent. One of the best ways to evaluate this is to practice in front of a mirror. You could also record video of yourself speaking, then ask someone to help evaluate your presentation. Most issues are easy to correct once the speaker is aware of and understands the problem.

The final tip is to vary your volume and pitch. If you speak in a monotone, your communication will be less effective because people will lose focus. Varying inflection and volume draws others' attention to what you say. For example, by slightly reducing the volume of your voice, you force others to listen harder.

Task Saturation

Task saturation is a condition that persists when you or your employees are so busy you cannot plan or lead effectively. It is an illness or virus that affects business owners, managers and employees who confuse activity with accomplishment. Everyone is constantly working in the business, but never on the business.

The negative effects of task saturation include creative stagnation, deflated morale, and diminished enthusiasm. We have seen many organizations lose their drive for success through task saturation. This is a very serious problem and one

Chapter 11 - Mastering Your Tasks

Become the master of your tasks

Some steps you should consider if you, your company or employees are infected with the task saturation virus are:

1. Make a list of every task you or your organization perform on a regular basis.
2. Analyze each task to see if it is still congruent or useful for the mission of the business. If a task has outlived its usefulness, consider eliminating the task.
3. Ask yourself whether any of your tasks could be done by a subordinate? If yes, consider delegating.
4. Are you focusing on what is urgent in your business or what is important? If you are focusing on the urgent, try changing your focus to the more important elements of running your business.
5. Ask yourself the question, "If I did not do this task, what would the consequences be?" If the consequences are small or negligible, consider dropping the task.
6. Allocate some time every day to plan and strategize.
7. Consider assigning someone in your organization to review and evaluate the level of task saturation in your organization. Or, hire a consultant to do the analysis.

that requires the cooperation of the entire company to overcome its effects. Don't allow yourself, or your organization to get bogged down by over scheduling.

The task saturation virus is exploding. You can, however, inoculate your business by becoming aware of the value of each and every task you and your employees perform within your business. Some of the major ways to eliminate task saturation are to eliminate mandatory attendance at mundane and unnecessary meetings, to effectively delegate tasks for the future, and to review existing tasks within your organization for possible cancellation or reallocation. Apply Dr. John Lee's "4 D's" to each task: can you **drop** the task? Can your **delay** the task? Can you **delegate** the task? If you must, then **do** the task.

> ### Take action don't resign yourself
>
> An entrepreneur was recently telling of his "stressed out" workforce.
>
> When asked what he meant by this, he explained they were working way too hard, and too many hours. He just did not want to hire temporary help for what he called the seasonal bulge.
>
> This attitude can be fatal to your business. Take required action to prevent overload.

▬ Loyalty vs. Productivity ▬

Can loyalty trade off for poor performance? Can great performance trade off for poor loyalty? No, neither of these alternatives is acceptable. However, if you have a very loyal employee who is not doing her job, then you have the obligation to sit down with this individual to work out a plan that will improve performance. It is critical, both to the employee's rehabilitation and the company's performance, that this meeting take place as soon as you notice the problem. Developing a specific

> ### Cultivate Loyalty
>
> *"The greater the loyalty of a group toward the group, the greater is the motivation among the members to achieve the goals of the group, and the greater the probability that the group will achieve its goals."*
>
> - Rensis Likert

plan to improve the worker's productivity is the key to the whole process. Keep it clean, simple, and easy to follow.

Dealing with an under-productive worker who has previously demonstrated his loyalty time and again requires that you devise a plan to motivate your employee and turn the situation around. Should this worker receive more leniency than a brand new employee? Of course! It is important to support those employees who have been with you in good times and bad. Hoping this employee problem will go away without you taking any action is wishful thinking. Refusing to address the issue will only grow the problem, possibly allowing it to spread and infect other employees in your organization. Act as quickly as practical. The longer the problem exists, the harder it will be to remedy.

Information Blockers

Many organizations have employees who block information. The motivation may be to feel important, to play the role of power broker or to protect their job. These information blockers are often self-righteous and view themselves as highly knowledgeable. They share only what is demanded and, even then, often grudgingly. To the casual observer, they appear bright and competent, but their information hoarding is often a sign of insecurity. Because they impede the full flow of information, information blockers have a negative impact on business performance.

The best way to deal with an information blocker is to talk to her directly. You need to make it clear that her actions are negatively affecting both the business and herself. Such employees need to be shown that information sharing actually increases their standing within the company. You must show them exactly how their actions are costing your business and clearly assert that information blocking can not be tolerated.

Chapter 11 - The 5 Clarities

The 5 Clarities

1. Have clarity of **purpose**. Success demands that we know specifically what we want. What is the goal to be accomplished?

2. Have clarity of **intention**. Why is the task necessary?

3. Have clarity of **responsibility**. Until responsibility for decisions and their results is accepted, it's impossible to know what works and what doesn't. Success comes from finding actions that accomplish the intended purposes, then repeating them over and over.

4. Have clarity of **priorities**. Decide on the most important attributes of a project or job (priorities). Define how these can be attained (goals). Set a time period for accomplishing these goals (macro time management). Decide how much time should be spent each day, or week, in attaining these goals (micro time management).

5. Have clarity of **acceptance**. If your employees can't clearly see themselves accomplishing the goals set before them, they are unlikely to attain them.

- Tim O'Brien

Cross Train & Systematize

Two ways to guard against a negative impact inflicted by an information blocker are to cross train employees and document procedures in precise detail.

Cross Training

- Have key employees cross train first each other, then at least one other person to an acceptable level of competence in each pivotal position in your company.
- Don't allow information blockers to wiggle out of participating.

Documentation

- Require each person in a critical position to detail the exact steps necessary to perform their major functions, tasks and subtasks.
- Next, have a cross-training employee following the steps exactly as written. If the process works, the details are sufficient. If the process breaks down, the experienced employee should continue revising the details until an untrained person can successfully follow the directions.
- Then, take all of these detailed procedures and put them into your company manual. (See Chapter 13) Review them annually and whenever procedures are added or dropped.

■ Confronting An Employee ■

There are two basic ways to deal with problem employees: do nothing or take action. Obviously, doing nothing does nothing. In fact, doing nothing usually makes the problem worse. Pretending the problem will resolve itself is tantamount to encouraging the behavior.

One effective way to approach a problem employee

is to ascertain what the real issues are, then address these in a private meeting. The sooner this meeting takes place, the quicker the problem can be solved or the decision to terminate the employee can be made.

Start the meeting by mentioning some positive contributions the employee has made to the organization. For example, you might begin with your gratitude to this employee for his five years of service. You should choose a concrete contribution to mention. For instance, you might thank this associate for the costs cuts he has facilitated in the purchasing department.

Next, explain the areas you are concerned about. You might say, "However, I am really concerned with the way you treat some of your subordinates and the number of work days that you have missed in the past two months." Some employees will be argumentative, but most will nod their head in agreement. Next, ask, " What can we do together to address this problem?" Then, work with

> ## Don't act blindly
>
> If you fear an employee may become hostile and destroy information or property, take preventive steps.
>
> Before speaking with them, back up and secure important data. Discuss the problem with a human resource expert and ask their advice on defusing any possible explosive situation.
>
> Sometimes the way you approach an employee makes all the difference in their reaction.

the employee to establish a timeline for correcting the problem.

It is vital that you work with the employee to develop clear and measurable performance goals to show his improvement. For example, "Your goal is to produce financial statements no later than the fifteenth of each month." You will also need to explain the consequences for failing to follow through with the agreement.

When you settle on the approach and details of the solution, write the plan down in sufficient detail to avoid confusion or misunderstanding, especially if there are significant digressions. To indicate mutual commitment, both parties should sign the document. It should then be placed in the employee's file. If you choose not to write down a formal plan, at least have the employee sign a statement confirming the meeting took place.

Close the meeting, by reminding the employee how much they have contributed to the business.

After the meeting is over, it is important to

Proper Resolution

1. Start the meeting with a positive statement.
2. Express your concerns.
3. Set specific, measurable performance goals.
4. Go over the details of solving problem.
5. Remind the employee how much he benefits the company.
6. Have the employee sign a statement and put this in his file.
7. Send the employee a letter summarizing the meeting.

summarize the major points in a letter to the employee. This will draw attention to the importance of the issues and possible consequences of non-compliance.

Termination

When you know you have to let someone go, make sure you have done your homework to prevent a backlash. Two common reasons for termination are violating the rules in the employee handbook and failing to live up to the job description. However, you are perfectly within your rights to let an employee go if you just cannot afford them anymore.

Take extreme caution

Chapter 11 - Termination

Often unpleasant, sometimes necessary

"I have had to terminate employees during my 35+ years of owning businesses.

Some were incompetent. Some I could no longer afford. Some just simply didn't fit in.

It might sound like a rationalization to salve my emotions, but I metabolize letting people go as an opportunity for them to find their perfect place in life. Their chance to find a way to serve others in a more fulfilling way than was available working for me.

Find your own way to think about difficult terminations. Don't take them personally."

- Tim O'Brien

to ensure that an associates termination is not perceived as discrimination (i.e. age, gender, religion, national origin, disability or race.) Defending a case of discrimination can cost tens, and sometimes even hundreds, of thousands of dollars.

Because of the potential for litigation, it is highly advisable to conduct your terminations under the guidance of a seasoned employment attorney. These individuals direct such terminations daily and can help protect you.

During the actual termination interview, it is important to have two people in the room to observe behavior, help remember details, and generally keep things running smoothly. First, thank the employee for their contribution to your company. Then, without blame or apology, simply tell them that, after today, they will no longer be employed in your company.

Frequently, it is useful to give an employee a choice between resignation and termination. Many prefer to resign as it allows them to avoid the stigma of having been released. Additionally, if an employee resigns she will not receive unemployment compensation, which keeps insurance rates down.

The next stage is to let the employee vent. However, you should not argue with the employee, even if he is blaming the company or you. This serves no useful purpose. Simply allow him to talk.

Tell the employee what, if anything, you are going to provide (severance pay, for example). Let her know when she must to leave the premises and what property needs returning. It is also useful to have your former employee sign a statement confirming the termination meeting took place. Finally, make sure you keep information about the termination confidential so as to protect the employee's privacy.

Crossing "T's" & Dotting "I's"

Keeping accurate records of employee behavior is vital.

1) Keep track of the actual details of each situation or activity. Work to find a balance between your memory and your notes. If you rely too heavily on memory, you will probably forget important details or remember something incorrectly. If you take too many notes, you will get bogged down. The idea is to keep track of critical points. Check lists are a helpful technique.

2) Keep a log of progress. Use the log as a reminder, and as a list of elements both completed and left to do.

3) For critically important details, use props, cues, or special reminders. Highlight an important detail in your log or use brightly colored sticky notes for different categories of employee behavior.

It is often advisable to turn off the employee's computer passwords during their termination interview to prevent damage to your computer system caused by revenge. Before the employee leaves, if possible and appropriate, it is wise to shake the former associate's hand and thank her for her service to the company.

Letting an employee go is very difficult, but it is best to take a straightforward approach. The sooner you do it, the better for both the firm and the employee.

One bad apple

Poison employees, those who are constantly negative, critical, sarcastic or intolerant can ruin the attitude of most everyone.

For the health and success of your company, you must consider terminating an employee with a poisonous attitude if there is no place to isolate him or her.

Don't allow *"one bad apple to spoil the whole bunch."* Work has to be enjoyable or it is unsustainable.

▬▬ Chapter Wrap-Up ▬▬

Chapter Wrap-Up

In this chapter you have learned:

- Speak clearly and at a pace employees can follow.

- Blanchard and Spencer's three "one-minute secrets."

- Your body language needs to match your words.

- To use Dr. John Lee's "4 D's" to help conquer task saturation.

- If there is a problem with a loyal employee's productivity, set up a meeting to discuss the issue and ways to resolve it, right away. Don't let the problem linger.

- The five clarities are purpose, intention, responsibility, priorities, and acceptance.

- Cross training helps your business counter information blockers.

- Do the necessary research to ensure your specific reasons for termination is not breaking any federal laws.

- It is wise to have to have two people witness the termination process.

FYI! PDF's of these forms are available online at:
www.osteryoungobrien.com
enter code: **OST+OBR=2010**

Chapter 11 - Problem Employees

Problem Employees

Do you have a problem employee? _____

Who is it? _____

Is the problem employee, a loyal or new employee? _____

What are they doing that is causing a problem? _____
_____
_____

Is this something that can be easily fixed ? _____

Using a scale of 1 - 10, (one being minor and ten being major) list how disruptive the problem is and why to the following:

You?   **1 2 3 4 5 6 7 8 9 10**
Why? _____

Managers?   **1 2 3 4 5 6 7 8 9 10**
Why? _____

Other Employees?   **1 2 3 4 5 6 7 8 9 10**
Why? _____

The business as a whole? **1 2 3 4 5 6 7 8 9 10**
Why? _____

The customers?   **1 2 3 4 5 6 7 8 9 10**
Why? _____

Chapter 11 - Problem Employees

Have you spoken with the employee, privately, concerning the problem? If no, why not? When will you? Set a date and time. _____

_____

_____

Did you discover the real issue? If yes, what is the issue? _____

_____

_____

Is there anything you can do to help the employee correct the problem? If yes, what will you do? _____

_____

_____

Did you give the employee a timeline for resolving this issue, or work with him to create one? If yes, what date is it to be resolved? _____

_____

Did you explain the consequences for not resolving the issue in a timely manner? If yes, what are they? _____

_____

_____

Have they taken any action steps to correct the problem? If no, what is your next action step? _____

_____

_____

 PDF's of these forms are available online at:
www.osteryoungobrien.com
enter code: **OST+OBR=2010**

Battling Task Saturation

Use the chart below, to help eliminate or prevent task saturation in your company, employees, and yourself. You can download and print a larger copy of this chart at *www.osteryoungobrien.com*.

	Task	Still Congruent?	Delegate?	Urgent / Important?	Consequences for not completing

Chapter 11 - Five Clarities in Action

Use the following questions to help with the tasks you are continuing after you have completed the chart on the previous page. These questions are based on the Five Clarities mentioned previously in the chapter.

What is the ultimate outcome to be accomplished for this task? ___

_____

_____

*Why is the task necessary?*_____

_____

_____

What are the most important priorities and goals of the project/ task? _____

_____

_____

How will the completion of these priorities and goals lead to achieving the ultimate outcome or completing the task? _____

_____

What is the timeline for the task? Are there milestone tasks to complete? If yes, what are they and when do they need to be completed? _____

_____

Who is responsible for completing the priorities and goals for the task? _____

*Is the employee comfortable with her role in this task? If no, why not? How can you increase the comfort level?*_____

_____

_____

The real purpose of these evaluations should be for the owner, manager, or supervisor to tell the employee how they are doing and whether they are living up to the expectations of the company. Another purpose should be for the supervisor to ask the employee, "What can I do to help make your job easier?"

–Jerry Osteryoung

Chapter 12

Delegation & Feedback

• •

Chapter At-A-Glance

By the end of this chapter you will know:

- The best way to delegate work to employees.
- How often you should evaluate your staff.
- How you should handle evaluations.
- What the Sandwich Approach is and how it can benefit you and your company.
- 360 evaluations, what they are and why you need them.

Mastering delegation multiplies productivity while saving time. Delegation is the ultimate "two-fer." Remember though, delegation is not abdication. The number one key to successful delegation is accepting full responsibility for the outcome of each delegated action or activity. As business owners and managers, we delegate tasks. We give instructions. We set standards and expectations. We set timelines. We negotiate prices and features. We never abdicate responsibility. When we delegate we still maintain control and final responsibility.

When you give an employee a task, assume nothing. Spell out every detail. Have examples, samples, and specifications. This sounds like work. It is. However, giving your employees a clear understanding of the tasks you expect them to complete is vital to their success in completing them well. After you've delegated tasks, it's important to give feedback on their progress.

Set up a regular, consistent, specific feedback system for your delegates to keep you updated and informed.

When assessing employee competence, the key is follow-up and feedback. Without feedback, there is no sense in going through the evaluation process. Many businesses which have no evaluation or feedback systems frequently end out in free-fall because the staff does not know if they are heading in the right direction. Employee evaluations really can make a difference in guaranteeing your expectations and desires are communicated to your workers.

> **Tips for Delegating**
>
> - Accept full responsibility for the outcome of delegated work.
> - Assume nothing.
> - Details! Details! Details! - Give plenty!
> - Set deadlines
> - Give examples/references
> - Give clarification. Make sure the project and what you want accomplished is understood.
> - Set up a feedback system to evaluate progress.

■Frequency of Staff Evaluations■

Annual evaluations are good, quarterly evaluations are better, but monthly evaluations are best. One problem with annual evaluations is they are typically the supervisor's perceptions based on the previous two weeks performance, since this is the freshest information. Consequently, these annual evaluations should probably be called "two-week" evaluations. Scheduling more frequent evaluations tends to produce more accurate results.

Employees need regular feedback. Scheduling evaluations a year apart leaves your employees unsure of whether they are on the right path and living up to your expectations. Your staff needs to hear from you frequently so they can deliver their best performance. Try to sit down with every employee under your supervision at least quarterly.

By analyzing the results of your meetings with your staff, you can develop an action plan for improvement. This plan should only be related to

things that the employee can actually change. For example, if an employee complains that his or her office is too small, there is very little that can be done. However, if the employee comments about a coworker's poor participation in team activities, action can be taken. It is important when going over these evaluations to separate what is controllable from what is not.

> **Power Quote!**
>
> *"Annual evaluations are one of the worst of all business practices."*
> -Jerry Osteryoung

Handling Evaluation

Don't be concerned that recommending more frequent evaluations will equal more paperwork. Rather, each manager should meet with staff members individually once a month on an informal basis. These meetings do not necessarily need to be about specific projects. It is a

time for you to hear what the employee's goals for the last month were, what he or she actually accomplished, and his or her goals for the next month.

Use this time to both evaluate how they are doing and to explore the resources they need to be more effective in their job. While

Chapter 12 – Sandwich Approach

this might sound like a huge investment of time, it really is an informal process that can be incorporated into your regular appointments. The bottom line is the more frequently you tell your staff how they are doing, the better the organization functions.

Jerry Osteryoung used this strategy with his staff each month. He took each individual staff member out for a meal giving him a chance to tell them how they were doing and giving the employee a chance to spend some time with him on a one-to-one basis. Some of the other points he covered were performance-related. If a staff member was not performing well in an area, they worked to correct those issues then and there rather than waiting an entire year before addressing the

The Sandwich Approach

Try to take the "Sandwich Approach" when speaking with an employee about problematic behaviors or attitudes.

1. First, tell the associate something good that they have been doing.
2. Then ask him how you and he can work together to solve any serious problems.
3. Finally, you should wind up by focusing on some other positive attribute of his work.

You need to work out a plan for improvement – one the employee understands and that has a definite time schedule. If the time period passes and there are still problems with the employee, then you need to terminate employment as soon as possible.

Typically, a problem employee has an effect on the entire morale of the business. The sooner that individual is removed, the sooner the morale of the business will improve.

issues again. Jerry also found it helpful to ask his staff if they needed any further resources. He made a special point of asking, "What can I do to be a better manager to you?" This isn't a popularity contest or a debate. He honestly looked for employee feedback so he could do his job better.

> **Power Quote!**
>
> *"Try to meet monthly with each of the employees you directly manage, if at all possible."*
>
> - Jerry Osteryoung

◼ Keep Employee Feedback in Mind ◼

If an employee submits an idea for a way to improve your management style or business functions, they must receive acknowledgment for their contribution. This is a simple yet, vital process. An employee who does not see their input taken seriously will cease to contribute. Ignoring your suggestions can only hurt your business; after all, one major incentive for employers to meet with their employees is to nurture ideas that will be beneficial to the company. If employees don't receive positive feedback, they will cease communicating ideas to you.

> **Power Quote!**
>
> *"You just cannot smile while telling an employee that there is a problem with their behavior. Make sure that your message and emotions are congruent."*
>
> - Jerry Osteryoung

360 Evaluations

There are other methods for evaluating your associates' performance. Another type of employee

> ## The Psychology of Optimal Experience
>
> This is a mini-review of a breakthrough book that holds one of the true keys to success and happiness. This is not folklore or wishful thinking. It is the result of 25 years of meticulous psychological research.
>
> The book is "Flow, the Psychology of Optimal Experience," published by Harper & Row. Its author, University of Chicago Psychology Professor, Dr. Mihaly Csikszentmihlyi (pronounced: chick-sent-me-hi) and his team of researchers wanted to know why some people grow, thrive and enjoy certain situations, while others experience burnout and depression, under the same circumstances.
>
> The Flow Research found five parts common to all Optimal Experiences.
>
> - A defined situation or challenge that one accepts.
>
> - Identifiable rules that govern behavior toward the challenge.
>
> - Specific goals that lead to mastery of the challenge.
>
> - Constant feedback allowing one to know the rate of progress.
>
> - Upon reaching a goal, new higher, more complex goals are set.
>
> Recall experiences you have when everything does Flow and goes smoothly. You will recognize these five criteria in those experiences. Then, look at experiences that don't Flow, and find which of the criteria are absent.
>
> The goal of Flow Research is to help us become increasingly developed as a person, and to help others we associate with grow also. This keeps life new and interesting.

Chapter 12 – 360 Evaluations

assessment for managers and staff to consider implementing is the 360° evaluation. The purpose of this strategy is to evaluate both upward and downward, as well as sideways.

A 360° evaluation involves compiling evaluations from four to eight people who assess the job performance of one employee. Evaluations are gathered from an employee's bosses, subordinates, and coworkers on the same level. You could also include customer feedback. It is one of the most effective ways to get good, solid information on an employee's performance. These evaluations and

comments are always conducted anonymously to ensure honest feedback. Besides being anonymous, evaluations are generally confidential in that they are only shared with the person

360° Evaluations

- Are done anonymously.
- Are confidential.
- Are shared with only the person who has been evaluated and the trusted person selected to review the results with them.
- Should be performed by four to eight people, generally superiors, managers, subordinates, and colleagues.
- Questions should involve communication, leadership, time management, production and management skills.
- Questions should also focus on personal development.

www.osteryoungobrien.com

Chapter 12 – 360 Evaluations

being evaluated. It is important that the person selected to review the evaluation with the employee understands that the purpose of the findings are to improve the employee's job performance. An outside, trained professional should facilitate this evaluation process.

Some of the standard questions asked in a 360° evaluation relate to communications, leadership, time management, production, managerial skills and personal development. For example, questions concerning communications typically deal with how the employee listens to others and whether he or she communicates effectively. Obviously, this type of evaluation only works well if your workforce is large enough to maintain anonymity in the evaluation process.

In order to use this system effectively, it is best to introduce 360° evaluations slowly and gradually move them into the entire organization. Something of this magnitude, if introduced in one fell swoop to the entire organization, will surely fail.

Chapter 12 – Face-To-Face Evaluations

Twelve Cornerstones of Face-To-Face Evaluations

1. Be conscious: when speaking with employees about their performance, remember to, "Say what you mean, and mean what you say."

2. Don't assume anything or take anything for granted. Ask questions to clarify.

3. Ask follow-up questions. This both shows interest and helps to avoid confusion or missed points.

4. Listen actively. Missing an idea or getting off the right path is inevitable if you only listen half-heartedly. Listen, repeat, and ask for clarification.

5. Look for clues. Often, people speak indirectly, for many reasons. Pay close attention to tone of voice, body language, and eye movements.

6. Think and analyze in layers. Look at what the employee has said topically. What is the overt intention behind the words or actions? Is there more going on below the surface?

7. Ask for help if you have doubts or confusion. Admit it and find a way to get clarification until you are comfortable.

8. Expect positive results. Be an optimist. Look for the good in situations. Also, be a realist, and analyze situations, not as a skeptic, but as an intelligent person.

9. Use multiple senses to help you convey messages to others and to analyze their communications with you.

10. Use multiple approaches. There are three major ways that people relate to the world: auditory, visual and kinesthetic. Try to tailor your approach to each employee's style.

11. Repeat yourself when necessary. Don't be redundant; however, if there is evidence your point was missed or perhaps even ignored, repeat yourself.

12. Ask the other party to repeat themselves when necessary. Clarity and accuracy are major goals of effective communication.

Chapter Wrap-Up

Chapter Wrap-Up

In this chapter you have learned:

- Delegation can be extremely beneficial if done correctly, but remember you are ultimately responsible for the outcome of any delegated work.
- How often to conduct evaluations. This varies depending on project time frames and critical benchmarks. For standard evaluations:
  - Annual = Okay
  - Quarterly = Better
  - Monthly = Best
- During evaluations you want to accomplish the following:
  - Determine the employee's goals last month.
  - What was actually accomplished?
  - Discuss discrepancies / refine process.
  - What are this employee's goals for the next month?
- The Sandwich Approach for handling problematic employees.
- 360 evaluations are performed anonymously by the employee's superior, subordinates, and colleagues. Be careful to keep this anonymous or problems could occur. Standard questions relate to:
  - Communications
  - Leadership
  - Time Management
  - Production
  - Managerial Skills
  - Personal Development

Chapter 12 – Delegation & Evaluations

Delegation

Of your routine tasks or current projects, which ones could be delegated? _____

_____

List the employees you can entrust with delegated responsibilities and match them to a task.

Employee   ### Task

_____   _____

_____   _____

_____   _____

What kind of feedback/communication system would work best for you and the employee for each delegated project? _____

_____

Evaluations

How often do you evaluate your staff? _____

*Do you currently evaluate each employee separately or as a group?*_

What is your new plan for evaluations? (frequency, style/type) _____

_____

Did you share something good they have done? How did they respond? _____

_____

Did you ask if there were any problems or confusions they need help in solving? How did they respond? _____

_____

Did you end with another positive attribute of their work? How did they respond? _____

_____

Chapter 12 – Feedback & Action Steps

Feedback

Do you have a feedback system set up between you and your employees? _____

One between your company and customers? _____

*You and your vendors?*_____

Are they efficient? How do you know? _____
_____

What could you do to make them more reliable and effective? _____
_____
_____

FYI! PDF's of these forms are available online at:
www.osteryoungobrien.com
enter code: **OST+OBR=2010**

Take-Aways and Action Steps

1. _____
_____
Completion Date: _____
*Results:*_____
_____

2. _____
_____
Completion Date: _____
*Results:*_____
_____

Chapter 13

The Last and the Shortest

● ●

Chapter At-A-Glance

In this chapter:
- Employee Practice Liability Insurance
- Company Manuals and Employee Handbooks

Currently, a nearly continuous stream of labor laws are being enacted to protect employees. Additionally, many plaintiffs' attorneys are very willing to step in and assist employees on a contingency basis. These two realities increase the likelihood of a company being sued over labor matters.

In 1994 the Equal Employment Opportunity Commission (EEOC) and related government agencies received 156 discrimination complaints. For the year ending 2003, there was a backlog of over 100,000 discrimination cases to be put before the EEOC. In a telephone survey of women, thirty percent claimed to have been sexually harassed in the workplace. Obviously, this growing trend toward suing employers is going to be very expensive for business.

Getting sued by a fired or disgruntled employee can be very damaging to your business both financially and emotionally. It has been estimated that defending an employee suit will cost more than $100,000 in legal fees even before it goes to trial. Additionally, forty percent of those cases that go to trial are won by the employee. Two extreme examples of

221

this are an international telecommunications company which settled a pregnancy discrimination case for $66 million, and a $15.6 million verdict rendered against a large food manufacturing firm for firing a 41-year veteran of the company accused of stealing a thirty-five dollar company telephone.

One solution to this problem is Employee Practice Liability Insurance or EPLI. EPLI will cover defense costs and pay any damages that a settlement or a court requires. Generally, these policies will cover you for discrimination, wrongful termination, sexual harassment, and work place torts(e.g. privacy invasion and defamation of character). There are normally limits on these policies between $500,000 and $5,000,000 with deductibles between $5,000 to $25,000.

Additionally these policies will cover you if a third party sues you for action by your staff (sexual harassment to a customer).

Recent annual quotes for EPLI have been around

Power Tip!

Business is hard enough without leaving yourself exposed unnecessarily to risks. Investigate insurance.

$2,000 for firms with forty to fifty employees. This is a very reasonable expense for this type of protection as liability exposure is very high.

Each policy for EPLI is different so you will need a good insurance broker to help you find the right policy for your company.

This is not an area to procrastinate. Make sure that you are protected from employee law suits. EPLI is a cost-effective way to insure that your firm has reduced or eliminated this risk.

Power Quote!

Would you try to assemble an important, intricate piece of machinery without a manual? Then don't try to run a business without one either.

Handbooks & Manuals

The first twelve chapters of this book covered all the areas we consider important regarding employees, from hiring, to training, to retaining to releasing them. One important area, mentioned many times but not yet covered is company manuals and employee handbooks. These are integral tools for a successful organization. In detailing rules, regulations, expectations and requirements, they become the basis for corporate behavior, compliance and culture. Their detailed entries remove ambiguity. They are also a ready reference for what is and is not acceptable.

Manuals and handbooks can't cover every possible scenario or situation a business will encounter. They can cover important areas that will help insure that you comply with the law and standard operating procedures. Educating managers and using a well-written employee manual greatly reduces the probability of a case going to trial. Additionally, a company manual and an employee handbook create a professional image for your company.

An employee handbook lays out, in very specific terms, the overall responsibilities of each employee, as well as the responsibility of the employer. Each new employee needs to sign a statement that they have received and read the manual and handbook. If this is a newly instituted manual or handbook then all existing employees need to sign a statement that they have read and understand them. Allow employees to read the handbook on company time. Also, employees need to sign-off on any revisions to the employee handbook.

There are some major items to avoid in your manual and handbook. Do not to promise continued employment. Do not promise that every workplace situation will be covered in the handbook or manual. Finally,

Chapter 13 – Critical Parts

do not promise to ALWAYS follow a specific disciplinary process.

If you already have a company manual and an employee handbook, that is good. Do you use them correctly? Are they up-to-date? When was the last time they were reviewed by your attorney? If you don't have a company manual and an employee handbook, where should you start? You could ask friends and associates who own businesses. If they do have them, ask to borrow them to help you create a manual and handbook for your company. You could

Critical Parts of Company Manuals & Employee Handbooks

Here are a few items you should remember to include in your company manuals and employee handbooks. For each section, include the consequences of breaking the rules or not adhering to company policy.

1. The basic rules of the business: attendance, tardiness, sick leave, vacation time, unpaid leave, pay, bonuses, pay schedule, overtime, part-time regulations, employee safety, work expectations, and paid holidays.
2. Prohibition of sexual harassment.
3. Include the phrase, "Subject to termination at any time without cause."
4. Include the phrase, "This Handbook should not be construed as a contract and may be changed at any time."
5. Conduct that can result in discipline and/or termination.
6. A procedure for settling disputes and handling complaints.
7. Dressing, grooming, and smoking policies.
8. Internet, e-mail and texting policies.
9. Alcohol and drug policies.
10. The procedure for and frequency of employee evaluations.
11. Company benefit plans (e.g. health, life and retirement plans).
12. Anti-discrimination policy.

Do NOT attempt to create Manuals & Handbooks without professional help and guidance! For an expanded version of these topics, please visit our website at *www.osteryoungobrien.com*.

check with your industry association to see if they have examples or guidelines. You could ask your attorney. A Google or Bing search will literally yield millions of results. There are prepackaged, basic versions available that you can customize. There are free templates you can download.

The important takeaway? Have company policy and employee behavior in writing. Remember the old saying, "If you think education is expensive, think about the cost of ignorance." It is not worth the risk involved to avoid developing a company manual and an employee handbook. You may feel the cost is expensive but the cost of not developing these documents could be prohibitive.

Conclusion

Employees are the essence of every business that isn't a "one-person show." Finding good associates is difficult. Motivating and retaining them is both an art and a science. The essential keys to personal and business growth are integrity, keeping your employees informed, keeping them in the development loop, allowing them a voice in what impacts them, compensating them properly, expressing your appreciation to them and managing inter-generational differences.

Contained, in that very long sentence, is both your challenge and your opportunity.

It is time to end this book now and send you on your way to a more successful relationship with your employees. Stay focused. Keep your dream always in mind. And remember, no matter what, there IS a way.

Parting Quotes!

"If you desire something with concentrated attention, if it does not yet exist, the Universe will manifest it for you."
    - S. Yukteswar

225

Chapter Wrap-Up

Chapter Wrap-Up

In this chapter you have learned:

- What Employee Practice Liability Insurance is and why it is important for your company.
- Why your company needs both a Company Manual and Employee Handbooks.

Company Liability Insurance

Do you have Employee Practice Liability Insurance? _____

If yes, when was the last time you reviewed the policy? _____

If no, have you done any research on how and where to get the insurance coverage your company needs? _____
_____

How much does/will it cost for specific business? Annually/monthly?
_____

What is covered under the policy? _____
_____
_____

Are there any gaps that will need to be covered by additional policies? How much do they cost annually/monthly? _____
_____
_____

Chapter 13 – Handbooks & Manuals

Employee Handbooks and Company Manuals

*What is the difference between an employee handbook and a company manual? Why do you need both?*_____

_____

_____

Does you company have a handbook and manual? If no, why not? _

_____

*Have the handbooks and manual been reviewed by an attorney? Did they recommend any additions or revisions? What were they and did you do them?*_____

_____

_____

Does your company use them correctly?If not, how can you correct the problem areas? _____

_____

Are they up-to-date? When was the last review? Last update? _____

_____

_____

*Do you set a good example for your staff by following your own rules and regulations from the handbooks and manual? If no, why not?*__

_____

_____

 PDF's of these forms are available online at:
www.osteryoungobrien.com
enter code: OST+OBR=2010

Chapter 13 – Take-Aways & Action Steps

Take-Aways and Action Steps

1. _____

_____

Completion Date: _____

*Results:*_____

_____

2. _____

_____

Completion Date: _____

*Results:*_____

_____

3. _____

_____

Completion Date: _____

*Results:*_____

_____

4. _____

_____

Completion Date: _____

*Results:*_____

_____

5. _____

_____

Completion Date: _____

*Results:*_____

_____

Index

Index

Index